Comics in Your Curriculum

Teacher-Friendly Activities for Making and Integrating Comics with Reading, Math, Science, and Other Subjects in Your Classroom

Written & Illustrated by
Richard Jenkins and Debra Detamore

Pieces of Learning

CLC0438
© 2008 Pieces of Learning
Marion IL
ISBN 978-1-934358-15-3

Table of Contents

INTRODUCTION

ONE STORMY NIGHT, I WAS UP LATE PLANNING MY WEEK.

HMMM... THESE BOOKS ARE NO HELP AT ALL!

I HAD BEEN LOOKING FOR IDEAS FOR USING COMICS IN MY LESSONS.

THEY'RE FINE TO LEARN HOW TO DRAW CARTOONY PEOPLE.

ZZZZ SNORT

OH WELL. I GUESS I CAN RE-CYCLE LAST YEAR'S LESSON PLANS.

CARTOONS!
DRAWING
PEANUTS

CLICK

ZZZZZ

-hmm-

OH! HELLO HANDSOME.

HELLO, MRS. FINKELSTIEN.

-OH- PLEASE CALL ME GRETA.

GRETA.

SAY! DO YOU KNOW HOW TO MAKE COMICS?

From the Authors

Each time I bring an armload of comic pages from our daily newspaper into my class to begin the day, my students rejoice. They don't say, "Oh boy, decoding, phonics, and comprehension!" But they do say, "Yea, comics!" Never mind they will be practicing all the skills that were just mentioned and that the students who have trouble reading get instant visual cues to help them. When a child has FUN learning, that is when things in the classroom really start to get good.

What could be better than watching a student enjoy reading comics? Even better is to watch a student write, draw, and publish their own comic strip. I have seen this happen in the classroom many times and am always impressed by the quality of the work the students produce.

The students take great ownership and pride in the comics they have made with their own hands. They don't mind proofreading, correcting, and rewriting. And, no matter how limited their writing or drawing skills might be, students feel successful when they complete their comics and have others who want to read them.

Debra Detamore

I have had a lifelong passion for creating comics. In 1997, I began my career as a Comic Book Artist. I was ecstatic. I was drawing comics "for real," and I was being published. Life was great. Then, I had the chance to begin my second career as a traveling Artist-in-Residence.

I was not sure what to expect from being a guest artist in classrooms. And, I was hesitant about losing some of the time and energy that went into my comics. But, much to my surprise, teaching students how to create their own comics became more than just another paycheck. In these residencies, I witnessed their enthusiasm and eagerness. I saw the wonderful, creative work they were producing. I found myself completely inspired and invigorated by their comics. I would show their work to my fellow cartoonists, who were also enthralled. All of this shared enthusiasm only made me work harder on my *own* comics.

Over the years, most of the teachers I have worked with have been eager collaborators. They recognized the immediate appeal of comics as well as the potential applications of comics in the classroom. Many of these teachers have shared their knowledge and showed me how to better instruct the students. Consequently, as I have continually produced comic books, I have also been creating activities and lesson plans for teaching comics.

All of this has revealed to me that I have a second passion, the sharing of comics with others. And that is the reason you find this book in your hands.

Richard Jenkins

THE ABC'S OF COMICS

HI, RICHARD! HOW ARE YOU DOING?

HEY, DEBRA.

WELL, I'M STILL NERVOUS. BUT I'M READY TO START.

YOU'LL DO FINE.

OH! I SEE THAT YOU ARE ALSO READY. SO....

CLICK

...BEFORE WE BEGIN, WE MUST FIRST CLARIFY WHAT COMICS ARE!!

WHAT IS HE TALKING ABOUT?! I KNOW WHAT COMICS ARE.

"SUPERMAN" AND "ARCHIE." RIGHT?

YES, GRETA. THOSE ARE COMICS. BUT COMICS ARE NOT "ARCHIE" AND "SUPERMAN."

"ARCHIE" DOES NOT DEFINE WHAT A COMIC IS.

JUST AS "GODZILLA" DOES NOT DEFINE WHAT CINEMA "IS."

GROONK

SO WHAT EXACTLY ARE COMICS?

* FOR MORE STUDY ON THIS CONCEPT, READ
"UNDERSTANDING COMICS" BY SCOTT McCLOUD

EXCELLENT POINT, GRETA. COMICS ARE MOSTLY A VISUAL ARTFORM. BUT...

...MUCH LIKE WORDS IN A SENTENCE, INDIVIDUAL IMAGES MAY BE JUXTAPOSED INTO A SEQUENCE. AND THE SUM OF THESE PICTURES FORMS A LARGER LINGUISTIC WHOLE.

WOW! SO COMICS ARE MORE OF A VISUAL LANGUAGE. *

RIGHT! NOW, READ THIS...

Chilly Surprise

by Wendy Pons

One bright and chilly morning, a boy awoke to his alarm. Reaching with his hand, he silenced the blaring clock. "Ugh! Time for school," he muttered. After stretching a bit, he took his bath.

When he was finished preparing for the day, he sat down to a bowl of hot oatmeal. "Aw, Mom," he cried, "lumpy oatmeal again?!" Patiently his mother replied, "Now Billy, this will keep you warm as you play out in the snow."

"What are you talking about?" Billy asked, confused. "I have school today." "Nope. School is cancelled," she said as she poured milk into Billy's glass. "Alright!" Billy exclaimed. Bring more of that oatmeal!" They both laughed.

NEXT, LET'S COMPARE THIS WRITTEN STORY...

...TO IT'S CARTOON VERSION ON THE FOLLOWING PAGE.

***** FOR A MORE IN DEPTH STUDY OF THIS THEORY, READ "EARLY WRITINGS ON VISUAL LANGUAGE" BY NEIL COHN

NOW WE...

DING DONG ♪♫

THERE SHE IS!

HEY, DEBRA!

HI, RICHARD! AM I LATE?

NOPE. YOU'RE RIGHT ON TIME.

IT'S ALL YOURS.

OKAY...

THE MOST OBVIOUS DIFFERENCE BETWEEN THESE TWO VERSIONS IS THE **PICTURES**.

Chi

ALL OF THE ACTIONS AND OBJECTS THAT ARE DESCRIBED BY "WORDS IN THE **WRITTEN** VERSION...

...ARE NOW SHOWN WITH IMAGES.

Chilly Surprise

IN COMICS THE PICTURES SERVE AS THE **NARRATOR**. AS A RESULT, THE CHARACTERS, SETTING, AND OBJECTS ARE MUCH MORE SPECIFICALLY DESCRIBED IN THE COMIC THAN THE WRITTEN STORY. FOR EXAMPLE....

AW MO LUMPY OAT

....

ALRIGHT BRING ON T OATMEAL

...LOOK AT BILLY'S FACE AND BODY. HIS EXPRESSIONS AND GESTURES ARE GIVING THE READER MORE CLEARLY DEFINED EMOTIONS. THESE VISUAL DETAILS BEHAVE LIKE ADJECTIVES AND ADVERBS, DESCRIBING BILLY AND HIS ACTIONS.

O.K., VERY INFORMATIVE.

NOW... HOW DO I APPLY ALL OF THIS IN MY CLASSROOM?

MEOW?

ALRIGHT GRETA...

...HERE'S A BRIEF EXAMPLE OF INTEGRATING COMICS INTO YOUR CURRICULUM.

FIRST, DECIDE WHICH SUBJECT MATTER OR SKILL SET YOUR ACTIVITY WILL NEED TO TARGET.

CURRICULUM

- LANGUAGE ARTS ➡ READING
- MATH
- SCIENCE
- SOCIAL STUDIES

⬇

VERBS Action Words

NEXT, INTRODUCE THE SUBJECT. SOLICIT SOME EXAMPLES FROM YOUR STUDENTS.

GIVE ME SOME ACTION WORDS.

WALK! **PLAY!** **SIT** **JUMP** **HIK** **RUN!** **HOP** **SWIM!** **DRIVE!**

THEN WRITE SOME "STORY STARTERS" THAT ARE GERMANE TO THE SUBJECT MATTER.

My name is _____.

I am __ years old.

I like to _____.

I don't like to_____.

I know how to _____.

USING THE BLANK PANEL TEMPLATES, INSTRUCT YOUR STUDENTS TO COPY THE STORY STARTERS.

NEXT, HAVE THEM DRAW PICTURES TO ACCOMPANY THE WORDS IN THEIR PANELS.

I like to hike.

COOL!

THEN HAVE THEM INK THEIR WORK. OR, IF YOU ARE SHORT ON TIME, PHOTOCOPY THEIR COMICS.

NOW THEY COLOR THEIR WORK AND I CAN HANG IT ON THE WALLS.

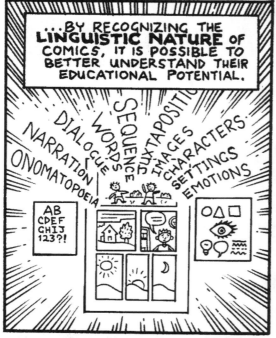

...TEACH YOUR STUDENTS HOW TO WRITE AND DRAW THEIR OWN COMICS.

...TO INTEGRATE OTHER CURRICULUM INTO THESE "STUDENT CREATED" COMICS.

...AND TO USE PREEXISTING COMICS IN ORDER TO TEACH OTHER CLASSROOM CURRICULUM.

The Purpose of
Comics in Your Curriculum

The goal of this book is threefold. First, it provides teachers with the tools that will enable students to write and draw their own comics. Second, it gives teachers resources so they can integrate other classroom curriculum into student-made comics. And third, the book offers activities that use pre-existing comics to introduce, reinforce, and practice many academic skills.

The activities in this book are intended to motivate all students, even those who may have difficulty reading. By using such a high-interest resource, students will have fun while they learn. Each activity begins with the students' prior knowledge, progresses through organized steps, and includes closure as well as tools and ideas for assessment.

Teachers who want to use the broad appeal of comics to teach and reach students will find this book a creative way to engage their classes in productive learning activities. This book shows that covering state and national standards for education can be fun and entertaining, too.

Children love to read comics because of their colorful and often funny content. Comics have been described as a "visual language." They are a great medium for communication and expression. So, both teachers and students will really benefit from the use of this book!

A BRIEF HISTORY OF COMICS

Since the first of our cave-dwelling ancestors decided to pick up a piece of charcoal and record the excitement of the hunt for food, man has left pictorial evidence showing how much we love to see pictures of the events that make up our lives. From Egyptian tombs to medieval tapestries, to the Sunday funny papers, there has been a need in us to put our stories into pictures, to leave a historical record of the small and grand accomplishments that affect us all.

Comic strips are defined as "a sequence of drawings, either in color or black or white, relating a comic incident, an adventure, or mystery story, etc., often serialized, typically having dialogue printed in balloons....." Comics can be silly or serious in nature and have changed oh so much since those days in the cave!

The history of our modern comics can be traced back to the late 1890s when they were originally created to increase the sale of newspapers. Over the next century, they were to change in appearance, but not in purpose, because even though comics are usually considered entertainment, they also are a reflection of our culture in America.

A comic called *The Yellow Kid* by Joseph Felton Outcault became the first to have a color added. It was of a little gap-toothed boy in a yellow "gown." By the end of the 1800s, comics were being printed in four colors.

The early 1900s saw the one-panel format of the political cartoon change into the multi-paneled strip with internal dialogue balloons with which we are now familiar. Beginning in 1905, Winsor McKay's *Little Nemo in Slumberland* took readers into the dreams of a young boy each week, and featured wild and unlikely adventures.

From 1912-1930, the focus of comics was on science fiction, which was a reflection of the industrial revolution. Buck Rogers made his debut in 1929. Following this, comic strips such as *Dick Tracy* and *Flash Gordon* came on the scene.

In 1938, the superhero was about to be born. Created by two teenagers and rejected by different publishers for six years, *Superman* finally hit the stands in DC Comic's *Action Comics #1*. With *Superman's* big success, the floodgates opened as other publishers created their own superheroes. During World War II, *Captain Marvel, Captain America* and others battled the Nazis and the Pacific Fleets. But with the end of the war, the superhero's popularity began to wane.

Next, true crime comics and women super heroes began to appear. In the 1950s comics took a turn to horror stories until The Senate Subcommittee on Juvenile Delinquency released a report very critical of comics. There were actually public burnings of comic books! By 1955, all comic publishers had greatly reduced their output. The Comics Code Authority was established, and publishers had strict rules they had to follow.

In 1956, Julius Schwartz, who was a big fan of science fiction, created a comic hero called *The Flash*, and a second age of super heroes was born. *Challengers of the Unknown, The Green Lantern,* and *The Justice League* became popular, and *Batman* and *Superman* flew high again. A second golden era of superheroes began.

Comics have continued to change since the '50s. They now cover a huge variety of subject matter and readability levels. Many are marketed for adults, with stories that are not appropriate for children. Yet, there are still many comics that are created for children and are age appropriate. There is a huge selection of comics that is useful in the classroom, and they are high-interest educational tools for the clever teacher.

Suitable Comics for Use
in the Elementary Classroom

The comic book market has grown up over the years. There are many comics that are created specifically for adults, as well as children. When you choose comics to use with students, be sure to read the book all the way through to look for words, violence, or other subject matter that is unsuitable.

The following comics may be found at regular bookstores, comic book stores, grocery stores and on magazine racks. These titles are created specifically for children and are all age appropriate.

Archie®
Batman Gotham Adventures
Batman Beyond
Betty and Veronica®
Bone Cartoon Cartoons
Cow and Chicken
Dexter's Laboratory ™
Jughead ®
Little Lit
Looney Tunes
Nickelodeon Magazine
Powerpuff Girls

Richie Rich
Samurai Jack
Scooby Doo™
Simpsons™
Sonic™ the Hedgehog
Space Ghost™
Spiderman
Star Wars® Adventures
Superman Adventures
Superfriends
Teen Titans

Some Helpful Books and Web Sites

Following is a list of excellent resources for teachers. Some are appropriate for use in the classroom, and some need to be edited for students. ALWAYS preview any comics, books about comics, or web sites that you might want to use in class.

100 Years of Comic Strips edited by Bill Blackbeard, Dale Crain & James Vance. This huge book has tons of examples of comics beginning in the early 1800s and ending in 1995. It's a great resource. (It was originally published in two separate volumes as The Comic Strip Century.)

The DC Guide to Penciling Comics by Klaus Janson.(5-6 graders)

From AARG! To ZZAP! by Harvey Kurtzman. This is a large, beautifully produced book about the history of comic books. It has lots of full-sized and full-color reproductions of old and recent comic books. WARNING - There are a couple of examples in this book which are inappropriate for young readers. You will need to carefully edit this one.

How to Draw Comics the Marvel Way by Stan Lee and John Buscema.

The Smithsonian Collection of Newspaper Comics edited by B. Blackbeard and M. Williams. This one is highly recommended! This enormous book has hundreds of full-color reproductions of comic strips dating from 1880 through 1980.

So You Wanna Be a Comic Book Artist by Philip Amara. (4-6 graders)

The Tenth Anniversary of Calvin and Hobbes by
Bill Watterson. This is a great resource! It
contains many beautiful color Sunday page comics as
well as dailies. In the front section of the book,
Watterson explains his creative process, the origin of his
characters, a brief history about comics, and which comics have
influenced him most.

Understanding Comics by Scott McCloud. (4-6 graders) This book is a
MUST for the serious cartoonist! It will be a bit too advanced for the
students, but it will be a great read for the teachers. This book will forever
change your perception of what comics are and their expressive potential.

www.comic-art.com A profusely illustrated web site chronicling the history
of comics. It has many full color examples from the 1880s through the
present day.

www.comicbookresources.com A news web site dedicated solely to comics.
It has previews and reviews of new books. Also featured are movies made
from comics.

www.cartoonnetwork.com The official web site for the Cartoon Network.
This site is loaded with online games and drawing lessons.

www.emaki.net This is the web site by Neil Cohn, a linguist scholar who is
doing new, exciting work about comics. The site explains his belief that
comics are a subset not of Visual Arts, but rather of Language!

www.marvelcomics.com www.dccomics.com & www.darkhorsecomics.com
These are all web sites for respective companies. Visit them to see previews
of new books, read submission guidelines, or view the fantastic art work.

www.reuben.org The website for The National Cartoonist Society

www.scottsmccloud.com This is the web site of the author of Understanding
Comics. It contains more essays about the form of comics. And it contains
lots of web comics.

An Introduction to the National Educational Standards

The lesson plans in this book are correlated to the National Education Standards. The authors have chosen those standards which they think apply to each lesson plan, but others may be appropriate also. A wonderful web site that lists and explains all of the National Standards is:

http://www.educationworld.com/standards/

At this web site you can also access all of the State Educational Standards.

In reading the National Standards, an explanation of the abbreviations and numbers used might be helpful. For instance, for the "History of Comics Internet Scavenger Hunt," the standards designated by the authors are:

Technology Standards
NT.K-12.5 Technology Research Tools
(This means: National Technology Standard, for Kindergarten-12th grades, Standard #5, which focuses on using technology research tools.)

Language Arts Standards
NL-Eng.K-12.8 Developing Research Skills
(This means: National Language Arts Standard, English language, for Kindergarten through 12th grades, Standard #8, which focuses on developing research skills.)

In all of the designations, the Curriculum subject is listed first. The grade level is listed second. The number of the standard for the skill being addressed is listed last. Here are some other abbreviations that might help:

NA-VA = National Art Standard, Visual Arts
NM-NUM = National Math Standard, Numbers
NSS-C = National Social Studies Standard, Civics
NS = National Science Standard

Lesson Correlations to National Educational Standards

History of Comics Internet Scavenger Hunt – page 29
Technology Standards
NT.K-12.5   Technology Research Tools
Language Arts Standards
NL-Eng.K-12.8   Developing Research Skills

Scrambled Comics – page 33
Language Arts Standards
NL-ENG.k-12.3   Evaluation Strategies
NL-ENG.k-12.6   Applying Knowledge

From Script to Comics – page 39
Lesson 1 - Writing the Script
Language Arts Standards
NL-ENG.k-12.4   Communication Skills
NL-ENG.k-12.5   Communication Strategies
NL-ENG.k-12.6   Applying Knowledge
NL.ENG.k-12.12   Applying Language Skills

Lesson 2 - Rough Draft Comics
Visual Arts Standards
NA-VA.k-4.1 & NA-VA.5-8.1   Understanding and Applying Media, Techniques, and Processes
NA-VA.k-4.2 & NA-VA.5-8.2   Using Knowledge of Structures and Functions

Lesson 3 - Drawing
Visual Arts Standards
NA-VA.k-4.1 & NA-VA.5-8.1   Understanding and Applying Media, Techniques, and Processes
NA-VA.k-4.2 & NA-VA.5-8.2   Using Knowledge of Structures and Functions

Lesson 4 - Inking
Visual Arts Standards
NA-VA.k-4.1 & NA-VA.5-8.1   Understanding and Applying Media, Techniques, and Processes
NA-VA.k-4.2 & NA.VA.5-8.2   Using Knowledge of Structures and Functions

Lesson 5 - Final Touches
Visual Arts Standards
NA-VA.k-4.5 & NA-VA.5-8.5   Reflecting Upon and Assessing the Characteristics and
                             Merits of Their Work and the Work of Others

Superphonics – page 50

Visual Arts Standards

NA-VA.K-4.6 & NA-VA. 5-8.6 Making Connections Between Visual Arts and Other Disciplines

Language Arts Standards

NL-ENG.K-12.3	Evaluation Strategies
NL-ENG.K-12.4	Communication Skills
NL-ENG.K-12.6	Applying Knowledge

Explain That Operation – page 53

Math Standards

NM-NUM.3-5.1 and NM-NUM.6-8.1	Understanding numbers, ways of representing numbers, relationships among numbers, and number systems.
NM.NUM.3-5.2 and NM-NUM.6-8.2	Understanding meanings of operations and how they relate to one another.

Language Arts Standards

NL-Eng.K-12.5	Communication Strategies

A Food Chain Comic – page 55

Science Standards

NS.K-4.3 & NS.5-8.3	Life Science
NS.K-4.6 & NS.5-8.6	Personal and Social Perspectives

Art Standards

NA-VA.K-4.1 & NA-VA.5-8.1	Understanding and Applying Media, Techniques, and Processes
NA-VA.K-4.3 & NA-VA.5-8.3	Choosing and Evaluating a Range of Subject Matter, Symbols, and Ideas
NA-VA.K-4.6 & NA-VA.5-8.6	Making Connections Between Visual Arts and Other Disciplines

Historical Happenings – page 57

Social Sciences: Civics

NSS-C.K-4.2	Values and Principles of Democracy
NSS-C.K-4.5 and NSS -C.K 5-8.8	Roles of Citizens

World History Standards

Any of the National Standards for World History may apply depending upon the time period studied.

Language Arts Standards

NL-Eng.K-12.5	Communication Strategies

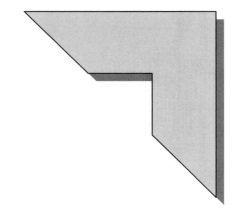

Clip Art Comics – page 60

Technology Standards

NT.K-12.1   Basic Operations and Concepts
NT.K-12.3   Technology Productivity Tools

Language Arts Standards

NL-ENG.K-12.4   Communication Skills
NL-ENG.K-12.6   Applying Knowledge
NL-ENG.K-12.8   Developing Research Skills
NL-ENG.K-12.12   Applying Language Skills

Fraction Comics – page 63

Math Standards

NM-NUM.3-5.1 & NM-NUM.6-8.1   Understand Numbers, Ways of Representing Numbers,
                                                      Relationships Among Numbers & Number Systems

Invention Comics – page 67

All National Standards listed for the "From Script to Comics" lessons and:

Language Arts Standards

NL-ENG.k-12.7   Evaluating Data
NL-ENG.k-12.8   Developing Research Skills
NL-ENG.k-12.12   Applying Language Skills

Science Standards

NS-k-4.5 & NS.5-8.5   Science and Technology
NS.5-8.6   Personal and Social Perspectives
NS.k-4.7 & NS.5-8.7   History and Nature of Science

Social Studies Standards

Individual to the invention studied and the time period in which it was created

Technology Standards

NT.k-12.5   Technology Research Tools

Alien Election Comics – page 69

Social Sciences: Civics

NSS-C.5-8.2   Foundations of the Political System
NSS-C.K-4.3 & NSS-C.5-8.3   Principles of Democracy

Comic Graphs – page 73

Math Standards

NM.NUM.6-8.1   Understand Numbers, Ways of Representing Numbers,
                                  Relationships Among Numbers and Number Systems

Language Arts Standards

NL-ENG.k-12.8   Developing Research Skills

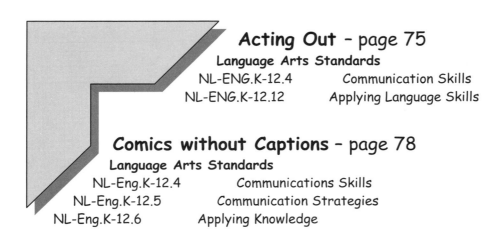

Acting Out – page 75
Language Arts Standards
NL-ENG.K-12.4   Communication Skills
NL-ENG.K-12.12   Applying Language Skills

Comics without Captions – page 78
Language Arts Standards
NL-Eng.K-12.4   Communications Skills
NL-Eng.K-12.5   Communication Strategies
NL-Eng.K-12.6   Applying Knowledge

Comic Collage – page 80
Visual Arts Standards
NA-VA.K-4.1 and NA-VA.5-8.1   Understanding and Applying Media, Techniques, and Processes
NA-VA.K-4.2 & NA-VA.5-8.2   Using Knowledge of Structures and Functions
NA-VA.K-12.3 & NA-VA.5-8.3   Subject Matter, Symbols, and Ideas

The "Save the World" Game – page 83
Language Arts Standards
NL-ENG.k-12.8   Developing Research Skills

Visual Arts Standards
NA-VA.k-4.1 & NA-VA.5-8.1   Understanding & Applying Media, Techniques, and Processes

Remember, the National Education Standards can be found on the Internet at: http://www.educationworld.com/standards/

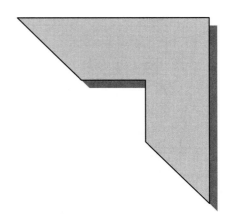

Lesson Plans

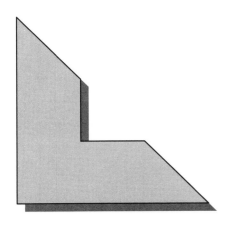

Helpful Hints

TRY SOME OF THESE USEFUL TRICKS.

Have students create a "comics folder" they can keep all year. Use this folder to store all of their comics' projects safely. Many of the activities require some worksheets. These include the Vocabulary of Comics page, as well as the Drawing Lessons pages and Tips on Creating Comics at the back of the book. Look for these in the table of contents.

Some lessons are longer, in-depth projects, while others are shorter and more narrowly focused. By keeping a folder, students can work on their comics as time permits and information they need is always at hand. The folder is also a great place for them to keep clippings of their favorite comics.

Always keep a good supply of newspaper comics and comic books in your classroom. Students will love reading them in their spare time, and they will be available to use as examples for lessons that are taught.

For younger students it may be helpful to have them draw their panels and comics on larger paper. This will give them more room to write dialogue and draw their pictures.

Try your hand at creating your own comic. This will give you an example to show students, and it will boost your own confidence and comfort level with this art form. Consequently you will be more experienced with the process of creating a comic, more familiar with the elements of comics, and more able to help your students.

We hope you will use the strategies and formulas we have laid out, and create your own comics integration projects!

History of Comics
Internet Scavenger Hunt
An Introduction to the
History of Comics

🏴 Grade levels: 3-6

🏴 Time: 1 class period

🏴 Lesson Plan Focus
   Using Technology to do Research

🏴 Correlation to National Education Standards
Technology Standards
NT.K-12.5   Technology Research Tools
Language Arts Standards
NL-Eng.K-12.8   Developing Research Skills

🏴 Objectives: Using computers, the students will learn about the history of comics by researching web sites to find the answers on the scavenger hunt worksheet.

🏴 Preparing for the Activity: The teacher will need to go to the web sites listed on the worksheet so they will be familiar with the historical background of comics their students will be learning about. These web sites could actually be printed out and displayed on poster board if desired. Depending upon the age of the students, you might want to bookmark the web sites the students will be using on each computer.

🏴 Introducing the Activity: This lesson is an introduction to the theme of comics. You might want to show some current comics with popular superheroes, and ask if anyone knows the year the character was introduced. (You should look this up before you ask!) Many will be surprised at just how long these comics have been around. Explain that the class will be using computers to do an internet scavenger hunt to learn more about the history of comics.

⚑ Materials
Copies of the "History of Comics Internet Scavenger Hunt" Worksheet
Pencils
Computers with internet access

⚑ Procedure
1. Hand out the worksheets and read the directions aloud. Call attention to the web site listed for the first section, then look on the second page for the other web site that will be needed.
2. Assist any students who have trouble navigating on the internet or have trouble finding the answers.
3. When all are finished, go over the worksheet aloud and discuss information that may have been new to the students. Ask them what they learned that they thought was most interesting or surprising.

⚑ Alternative Use of This Lesson
We understand that all classes do not have access to enough computers so all students could work at the same time. This could be used as an anchor activity in classes with just one computer, and students could work in pairs and take turns to do the worksheet.
Having no computer access changes the focus of the lesson, but the teacher could still look up the information and use it in a presentation to the class about the history of comics.
Use "The History of Comics Internet Scavenger Hunt Rubric" on page 124.

⚑ Answers to the Worksheet Questions
1. Comics were "a tool to draw customers to the Sunday edition of the newspaper."
2. Winsor McCay created "Little Nemo in Slumberland."
3. Some "science fiction" comic characters were Buck Rogers of the 25th Century A.D., Flash Gordon, and Tarzan.
4. Answer: The first modern comic book.
5. Answer: Superman
6. Answer: The Batman
7. Answer: The bottom dropped out of the comic book market.
8. Answer: The Flash
9. Answers: the Incredible Hulk, the Mighty Thor, Iron Man, the X-Men and the Avengers.
10. Answer: The Bronze Age

Name: _____   Date: _____

Ready to find out some interesting information about comics?
Go to the web site www.comic-art.com and find the answers to these
questions about their history.

When you get to this web site:
~Click on 'History of Comics'
~Then click on 'A Pictorial History of American Sequential Art Part 1'

1. Why were comic strips originally created?

_____

_____

_____

2. In 1905, the comic strip "Little Nemo in Slumberland" changed
the way comics had been written. It was one of the first strips
to begin a story and continue it through several weeks.
It was written and drawn by a man named_____.

3. Some of the first comic strips of the early 1900s were about
science fiction. Name two of them: _____

_____

_____

4. In 1933, Eastern Color Press came up with the idea of printing
an 8 page comic section that could be folded into smaller pages.
What was the result of this? _____

_____

5. What was the name of the first superhuman comic character who had super strength and powers?_____

Now, go to another site. Go to:
http://www.techdock.com/History/the_early_years.htm

Click on the section that says "The Golden Age."

6. In May 1939, Detective Comics # 27 introduced what caped crusader? _____

7. From the 1940s to the 1950s, what happened to the comic book market? _____

_____

_____

Go to the next page, "The Silver Age".

8. Which comic hero brought super heroes back to comic books, in the book Showcase #4? _____

9. Spiderman was introduced by Marvel Comics in the 1960s. Name another superhero from this time period. _____

_____

Go to the next page.

10. What are the years in comics from 1970-1990 called?

_____

Scrambled Comics
A Sequencing Activity

⚑ Grade level: 3-6

⚑ Time: 30-45 minutes

⚑ Lesson Plan Focus
   Sequencing in Reading

⚑ Correlation to National
   Education Standards
   Language Arts Standards
   NL-ENG.k-12.3 Evaluation Strategies
   NL-ENG.k-12.6 Applying Knowledge

⚑ Objectives: Students will put the mixed up panels of a comic strip into the correct sequence so the "story" makes sense. They should understand a good story needs a beginning, a middle, and an end.

⚑ Preparing for the Activity: Gather samples of the daily and Sunday newspaper comic strips. Cut out the comic strips, and make photocopies of them for the activity. Keep the originals for your reference.

Then, cut the copied strips apart, and place all the panels for each strip into numbered envelopes labeled with the name of the strip. You will need one comic strip for each student, or you can have students work in pairs, and reduce the total number of comic strips you will need.

⚑ Introducing the Activity: Ask the students if they read the comics in the newspaper, and if they do, which ones are their favorites. Then ask, "What is the purpose of most comics?" (They are mainly to communicate an idea, to entertain, or to be funny).

Can students tell you where the funny part or the "punch line" usually is located in a comic? (It is usually at the end.) Discuss with the class whether it would make sense for the punch line to be at the beginning or the middle of the comic.

If possible, make an overhead transparency of a comic that has been cut apart and scrambled. Have the class put it in order to demonstrate the skill.

⚐ Materials
Copies of the comics Vocabulary page 99
Prepared scrambled comics in numbered envelopes
Transparency of a scrambled comic (See the accompanying page.)
Notebook paper and pencils
A master list of comics and what number of envelope they are in

⚐ Procedure
1. Hand out copies of the comics Vocabulary page. Go over the terms, and tell students they will be referring to the sheet, and they need to keep it in their comics' folder. Point out examples of each term on the comic on the overhead.

2. Explain to students they will be reading comics panels and putting them into the correct sequence so the story and pictures will make sense.

3. Tell them they will label their notebook papers with the number of the envelope their comic is in. Once students have the comic put in order, they should raise their hands so the teacher can check their work.

4. Students may need clues to help them. Guiding questions such as "What comes after a problem? (a solution), might be helpful. Then, once they have put the comic in correct sequential order, they will write the words from the panels on their papers. In this way, they will be checking the story to see if it makes sense, and the teacher will be able to check the papers to see if the student has done the activity correctly. They will also be writing the comic **script** that the artist created before he drew the pictures for the comic.

5. When the student finishes with one comic strip, have them trade with someone else and do another strip. You can choose how many you would like them to complete.

⚑ Assessment

The teacher should visually check the students' work as they are doing the activity. The written work may also be graded to see if the students have successfully completed the skill of sequencing.

⚑ Closure

Have students tell you the three parts of a comic story. (They should answer," The beginning, middle, and end.") The story would be very confusing if it was out of sequence, and the punch line would be ruined. Tell them the skill they have practiced in this lesson will be very helpful when they get to create a comic **script** for their own comics.

Tips:

~If a student has a comic panel that has no words, they can just write that is was "blank."

~You could laminate your scrambled comics, and reuse them with multiple groups.

⚑ Extension

Take a well-known story (<u>The Three Little Pigs</u>, for example) and divide this story into its individual sentences. Have students work in groups to illustrate a comic panel to go with their particular sentence. Next, have students write their sentence at the top of their panel. Finally, put the created comic panels into their correct sequence.

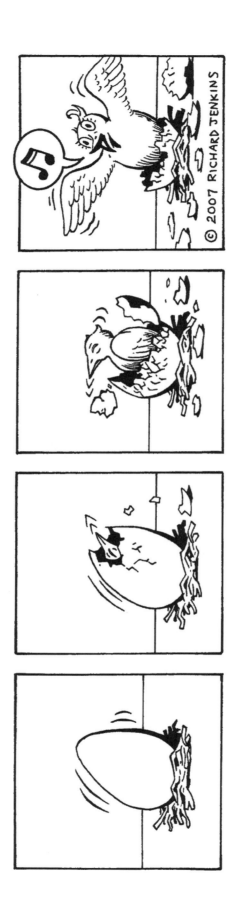

38

From Script to Comics
A Five-Step Lesson for Writing and Drawing Comics

⚑ Grade Level: 3-6

⚑ Time: 6-10 hours. With the emphasis on revision, each of these stages must be evaluated by the instructor. Remind students their comics will be seen by other students, so they'll want to do their best.

⚑ Lesson Plan Focus
English and Art skills

⚑ Correlation to National Education Standards
Language Arts Standards
NL-ENG.k-12.4	Communication Skills
NL-ENG.k-12.5	Communication Strategies
NL-ENG.k-12.6	Applying Knowledge
NL.ENG.k-12.12	Applying Language Skills

⚑ Objectives
Students will learn a creative writing process using words and pictures together. They will practice writing a rough draft, proofreading, correcting and revising, and writing a final draft. They will also do rough draft and final draft artwork goes along with their stories.

⚑ Introducing the Activity
Hand out comics that have been cut from the newspaper, and have students tell which strips the panels are from, the characters' names, and if possible the artists' names who created them. Have students tell where they see comics and which ones they like to read. Draw on their prior knowledge to have them discuss how comics are useful in everyday life.
It might be helpful to have students do the "Scrambled Comics" activity before proceeding with this lesson.

⚑ <u>Materials</u>

Notebook paper	Black 'rollerball" ink pens
Pencils	Black markers (thick and fine point)
Erasers	White correction fluid
Typing paper	Coloring pencils
White construction paper	Rulers

Class copies of the following worksheets:

Comics Vocabulary p. 99	Blank Panel Layout pages p. 93-97
Drawing Handouts	Bubble Letters Handout p. 110-111

From Script to Comics Handouts (Optional) p. 101

Samples of each step in the creative process (Student examples of
   Writing, Rough Draft Comic, and Final Draft Comics)

⚑ <u>Assessment</u>

Use the "Student-Made Comics Rubric" on page 116.

Lesson One
Writing the Script

🏴 <u>Time</u>: 30-60 minutes

🏴 <u>Materials</u>
Notebook paper and pencils.
Comics Vocabulary Handout p. 99

🏴 <u>Procedure</u>
1. Instruct students to write short stories (4-8 sentences). Their story may have any subject, mood, setting, or style. Emphasize whichever Language Arts elements you need for your curriculum. Some students may need a story starter to help them begin writing. See the list below for ideas.
2. When their rough draft writing is done, they may trade papers and proofread each other's work, but the teacher will also need to proofread these. The story will become the **script** for their comic.
3. After stories are complete, review the vocabulary of comics. Remind them that in comics, some of the words may be replaced with pictures or shown by the expression on a character's face.

🏴 <u>Assessment</u>: Students should have written a short story with a beginning, middle, and end. Their spelling and grammar should have been checked and corrected.

Story Starters:

" It was a warm day at the city dump, when Andy and Joe saw something shiny. . . "

"Mary looked up into the sky and yelled, "Wow! That looks like a . . . "

"Ashley and Tommy were eating in the cafeteria when they noticed something weird about their mashed potatoes . . ."

"Going inside the cave had been Johnny's idea. But, Max got a little scared when he saw the glowing eyes up ahead and knew it was a . . ."

"Callie threw her fishing line into the water. When she pulled it out . . ."

Lesson Two
Rough Draft Comics

⚐ Time: 1-3 hours

⚐ Materials
   Written stories
   Bubble Letters Handout p. 110-111
   Typing paper
   Panel Layouts Handout p. 112
   Pencils
   Erasers
   NO RULERS

⚐ Procedure
1. Explain to students they will be drawing their comic **two** times. First, they will do a rough draft, or a practice comic. (Show them the Sample Rough Draft Comic). This process, called **Revision**, will enable them to plan and organize all of their pictures, panels, words, and captions **before** they spend hours drawing their Final Draft Comic.

2. Also, tell them this rough draft comic will be reviewed by you, to ensure they have clarity and creativity. Inform them you will be marking on their rough draft drawings.

Step One: Panel Layout
(Preprinted panel templates may be used for this step)

Pass out the examples of different Panel Layouts. Give students a few minutes to look them over.

On the chalkboard, demonstrate a panel layout with gutters. Remind the students that in our culture we read from left to right, and top to bottom. They may use unusual panel layouts and shapes, as long as the reader will be able to follow the story.

Next, using pencils and white typing paper have the students sketch out their desired panel layouts. They should not exceed 5 - 7 panels per page.

They should have <u>about</u> one panel for each sentence in their story, although some panels may have more than one sentence.

Check layouts to make sure students include gutters between panels and around the outside of their panels.

Also check for "readability" of their panel layouts. Sometimes arrows or numbers will help to clarify the sequence of their panels. They must have **large** panels and **small** gutters because they will need plenty of drawing space inside their panels.

Step Two: Title Design

Pass out the Bubble Letter Handout, and have students read over them. Have students sketch a title design inside the first panel of their layouts. Instruct them to use a larger and different lettering style than the rest of their comic. Block or bubble letters work well here.

Step Three: Sketching

Tell the students to begin writing their comics by moving over to the next panel and copying their first sentence from their story at the top of it. Now have them draw a picture that coincides with these words. Remind them to KEEP IT SKETCHY, and only outline items they are drawing and use stick people. (They are just PLANNING their comics). Then, have them proceed to the next panel and add the second sentence from their stories, add a picture, and so on.

Encourage students to add speech, thoughts, and sounds to their pictures. They will use these elements of comics to enhance and clarify their stories.

Remind them the gutters must remain <u>empty</u>.

Changing viewpoints in their pictures will make the students' comics more interesting. They can try drawing characters from different angles, pulling up close to a character's face, or just showing a part of something in the picture. Also they could draw a view from far away where the characters look small. Or, a close-up view where we see just the upper part of the characters' bodies.

Step Four: Revision

After they have finished sketching their rough draft comics, proofread student work for spelling, clarity, readability, organization of the literal and visual information, and creativity.

As you review their rough drafts, you should be able to discern whether the pictures are occurring inside or outdoors, if there are different-sized characters and objects to show scale, if the scene changes from panel to panel, and whether it is night or daytime.

Have students make necessary revisions.

⚑ Assessment: Panels should have gutter space between them, and the title design should be creative and clear. Pencil sketches should illustrate the story. All words should be readable.

Tips:

~Give students a deadline for their rough drafts.

~Tell them to draw lightly so erasing is easier.

~Students should ALWAYS write the words before drawing the surrounding captions (word balloons). Most of the words should be horizontal and near the tops of the panels.

~Check that the sequence of speaking is clear. Captions at the tops of the panels are read first, the one beneath it is read next.

~Most panels should have some kind of background to make the pictures look complete.

Lesson Three
Drawing

⚐ <u>Time</u>: 2-4 hours

⚐ <u>Materials</u>
Rough Draft Comics
White <u>construction</u> paper OR copies of
   Blank Panel Layout pages, if used in the
   Rough Draft, on white construction
   paper
Pencils
Erasers
Rulers
Drawing Handouts

⚐ <u>Procedure</u>
1. Using their revised rough drafts as their guide, instruct students to redraw their final comics. But, this time they will be adding all of the interesting details, using their rulers, and making further revisions in their pictures and words to clarify and enhance the comics. But, NO coloring yet.

2. Remind them to refer to the Drawing Handouts for ideas.

3. Make sure students draw any repeating characters or props in a consistent manner. This way, the reader will not get confused.

4. Remind them to draw LIGHTLY. It is easier to erase mistakes if the drawing is not too dark.

5. Students may add or subtract elements from their work if it doesn't cause confusion in the stories.

6. Proofread all work again when drawings are finished.

▶ <u>Assessment</u>

Student comics should have been copied from the rough draft onto construction paper or Blank Panel Templates with minimum changes. They should be neat and readable.

Tips:

~If pencil smudging occurs, have the student place a sheet of typing paper underneath their drawing hand. They should not color anything in black with their pencils. That will be done in ink later.

~Check comics to see that students are writing their lettering first, then drawing the caption bubble around it. In their eagerness, they often forget this.

Lesson Four
Inking

⚐ <u>Time</u>: 1-3 hours

Even the most careful artist will see their pencil drawing fade as they work. Inking is a way of ensuring all students' pictures and words remain visible and legible to the reader. This is also important if you intend to make copies of the comics for a class book or other publication.

⚐ <u>Materials</u>
   "Penciled" Final Draft Comics
   Fine point black "rollerball" pens -NOT "ball point" pens
   Fine and thick point black markers
   Bottles of white correction fluid

⚐ <u>Procedure</u>

1. Using the thick or fine black <u>marker</u>, the students will "ink" (trace) over all of their pictures & panels.

2. Using the fine point black "<u>rollerball' pens</u>, the students are now ready to ink all of the lettering, the captions, and all of their drawings.

3. When inking is complete, the students will "clean up" their work by erasing all visible pencil lines and smudges.

4. White correction fluid can be used when a mistake is made in ink.

PROOFREAD ALL WORK ONCE AGAIN.

⚑ <u>Assessment</u>

Everything that is written and drawn in the comic should have been traced over with a black ink pen.

Tips:

~Encourage students to add variety in their inking. Have some panels with very little filled in with black, and some panels with a lot of black.

~Instruct students to ink carefully and deliberately. This definitely affects their finished products.

~If you are short on time, you can skip the inking stage and photocopy their Final Copy Comics. This will darken all of their lines and letters, thus ensuring the clarity and legibility of their comics. As with INKED comics, when they color the photo copy comics, their lines and letters will not smear.

Lesson Five
The Final Touches

⚑ Time: 1-3 hours

⚑ Materials
Inked or Photo Copied Final Comics
Colored pencils

⚑ Procedure
1. As students begin coloring their comics, remind them to keep the gutters clear. They should maintain the clarity of their characters by repeating the colors on their clothing from panel to panel.

2. Most of the captions should be kept free of color. Exceptions to this are the title, sound words, and other occasional captions. If you have a student who really wants to add color to their captions, limit them to the lighter colors so their lettering will not get lost.

3. Throughout their comics, encourage students to mix and blend their colors. They should try to add variety to the colors they use.

⚑ Assessment
See the sample grading rubrics in the last section of the book. Readability and creativity of the comics are the most important points by which to grade. And, students should have been able to work through the process of writing, revising, and rewriting successfully.

The students' comics should be ready to put on display or to share with other readers in some way.

⚑ Closure for the Entire Assignment
Have an oral review of the processes involved in creating and publishing a comic with the students. They should understand comics are a visual language that communicates ideas and feelings to the reader.

Remind students comics are a fun form of communication and are themselves a reward for the hard work goes into them.

Superphonics
A Reading and Language Activity

⚐ Grade levels: 1st and up

⚐ Time: 1 class period

⚐ Lesson Plan Focus: Sound Words in Reading and Language

⚐ Correlation to National Education Standards:

Visual Arts Standards

NA-VA.K-4.6 & NA-VA. 5-8.6   Making Connections Between Visual Arts and Other Disciplines

Language Arts Standards

NL-ENG.K-12.3   Evaluation Strategies
NL-ENG.K-12.4   Communication Skills
NL-ENG.K-12.6   Applying Knowledge

⚐ Objectives: Students will discover, recognize, and read sound words found in comic strips. They will associate the way the sound word is graphically written with the sound it is supposed to represent.

⚐ Preparing for the Activity: The teacher will need to get copies of comic books and comics from the newspaper to be used in the activity.

⚐ Introducing the Activity: Ask your class if they have ever read the comics in the newspaper or a book. Most will say they have. Next, ask if they have ever noticed words in those comics that are "sound" words.

Explain comics are unique types of reading material, because they contain "sound effects" books usually don't have. (Words representing sounds - Onamatopoeia - could be brought into the lesson when used with older students.) Today students will be looking through comic strips to find the "sound effect" words the artist has used.

Tell the class they will be paying special attention to the way words can be written so readers can really understand how they are meant to be said.

Begin by saying the word "pow" softly. Ask the students if that seems like the way the word was meant to sound.

Have the group say "POW" loudly, to better convey the meaning of the word. Write the first "pow" on the board in lower case letters. Write the second "POW" on the board in upper case letters with lines coming out all around it. (You can ask the class to help you draw the word correctly so its meaning is shown.)

 Materials
   Comics, examples of sound effects from comics
   White drawing paper
   Pencils and erasers

 Procedure
Tell the class they will be looking through comics for "sound effect" words. When they find one, they should keep it marked because they are going to share it with the class.

1. Hand out the comics and allow exploration time. Students will want to read some of the comics before settling down to find their "sound effect" words. The students may work in groups or individually, depending on their ages,
2. Set a timer or call time when all students have had an opportunity to read the comics and find a sound word.
3. Go around the room and have each student read the sound word they have found. Have them read it with expression.
4. Hand out white drawing paper, and have each student write their sound word at the top of it, as the word is written in the comic. Underneath the word they should include a picture of the character who is saying the word.
5. The work should be done in pencil first, then gone over with markers or crayons. Be sure each student has signed their page.
6. Pass the pages around so all students get to see them.

⌐ Assessment

The student should correctly identify and reproduce the sound word from the comic onto a sheet of paper. He or she should be able to express the word with the meaning graphically represented in the comic.

They should complete their page with an illustration.

Use the "Group Comic Activity Rubric" on page 115.

⌐ Extensions

~Have students put the pages into alphabetical order and bind their pages into a "Superphonics" book, and share it with other classes.

~Older students could be given a letter of the alphabet their sound word has to start with. If they cannot find an example of a sound word that begins with their letter, they have to come up with a creative one of their own. (A dictionary would come in handy here!) They should also be better able than younger students to create and draw a complete character on their page that goes along with their "sound effect."

Explain That Operation
Creating an
Informative Math Comic

⬤ <u>Grade levels</u>: 3-6

⬤ <u>Time</u>: 1-2 class periods

⬤ <u>Lesson Plan Focus</u>: Demonstrating
  Understanding of a Math Concept, Art

⬤ <u>Correlation to National Education Standards</u>

Math Standards

NM-NUM.3-5.1 and NM-NUM.6-8.1	Understanding numbers, ways of representing numbers, relationships among numbers, and number systems.
NM.NUM.3-5.2 and NM-NUM.6-8.2	Understanding meanings of operations and how they relate to one another.

Language Arts Standards

NL-Eng.K-12.5	Communication Strategies

⬤ <u>Objectives</u>: The student will be able to explain the concept of a math operation through the creation of an informational comic.

⬤ <u>Preparing for the Activity</u>: Find examples of informational comics to show the class. Often these are found on cereal boxes, baking mixes, and in assembly directions for different items. <u>Odyssey</u> Magazine runs an informational comic called "Stargazing with Jack Horkheimer" that would be a great example.

⬤ <u>Introducing the Activity</u>: Remind the students comics can have many uses. They can tell a story, be entertaining and funny, or they can be factual and informative. Ask the class if they can think of any informational comics. Show the example you have found.

⬤ <u>Materials</u>
  Copies of a Blank Panel template p. 92-97   pencils and erasers
  Rulers   colored pencils
  White correction fluid

⚑ Procedure

1. Because in this lesson students explain a math operation, you should decide if you want to use this activity as a re-teaching tool or for assessment. You may want to assign an operation or math term for the students to explain, or allow them to choose their own. Once that decision is made, the goal is for them to pretend they are teaching someone who has never heard of the idea before.

2. Explain this comic will be written in the first person and in it the student will be talking directly to the reader. They may wish to draw themselves as the main character or to create a character to do the "teaching" in the comic.

3. Each student should choose a blank panel template page with the number of panels that correspond to the number of steps in their explanation. They could also draw their own panels if none of the templates have the needed number. Remind the students they should write and draw lightly in case they need to erase and correct. You may wish to have the students write their comic script out on notebook paper before they put it onto the template page so you may check for clarity and errors.

4. Remind students to write dialogue first in the panels of the comic and then to draw the bubble around the words.

5. When finished and checked, students should ink their comics. They may also color them if desired.

⚑ Assessment
The student should have been able to explain and illustrate the math concept in a way that is understandable. The comic should be completed and readable.
Use the "Explain That Operation Rubric" on page 122 or the "Student-Made Comics Rubric" on page 116.

⚑ Extension
Have students create a comic with a math problem as the solution to the crisis in the story.

© Pieces of Learning

A Food Chain Comic
A Cooperative Science Activity

▶ <u>Grade levels</u>: 3-6

▶ <u>Time</u>: 1 class period

▶ <u>Lesson Plan Focus</u>: Science and Art

▶ <u>Correlation to National Education Standards</u>

Science Standards
NS.K-4.3 & NS.5-8.3   Life Science
NS.K-4.6 & NS.5-8.6   Personal and Social Perspectives

Art Standards
NA-VA.K-4.1 & NA-VA.5-8.1 Understanding and Applying Media, Techniques,
                             and Processes
NA-VA.K-4.3 & NA-VA.5-8.3 Choosing and Evaluating a Range of Subject Matter,
                             Symbols, and Ideas
NA-VA.K-4.6 & NA-VA.5-8.6 Making Connections Between Visual Arts and Other
                             Disciplines

▶ <u>Objectives</u>: Students will be able to correctly identify the links of a completed food chain and illustrate a group comic showing that information.

▶ <u>Preparing for the Activity</u>: Make name tags showing an animal or plant in the food chain for each student. Examples are listed at the end of the lesson.

▶ <u>Introducing the Activity</u>: Review a science lesson about food chains. Ask students to give examples. Make sure they have a good understanding of the order of a food chain.

▶ <u>Materials</u>
   Nametags
   White typing paper
   Pencils and erasers
   Crayons or markers

⚐ Procedure

1. Hand out a food chain nametag to each child for them to wear. Next, have them get up and group together with others who will complete their food chain. The teacher will need to check each group to make sure all have chosen correctly.

2. Once in their groups, have students sit together. Give each of the students a piece of white typing paper, and have them illustrate their role in the food chain. These sheets of paper are the "panels" of their comics. Have them color their pictures with crayons or markers when finished.

3. To make comics of these, give each group a large sheet of colored butcher paper to glue their pictures on. Remind them they must place the pictures in the correct order when they illustrate their food chain. Encourage them to experiment with placement of their pictures. For instance the comic could take the shape of a triangle instead of a straight line.
Ask students to come up with a way to show what direction the comic should be read. Visual cues such as arrows could help.

4. Have students add narration boxes at the tops of their papers and captions so their food chain parts can speak. These can be humorous and still reinforce the science lesson.

5. Hang the finished Food Chain Comics out in the hall for others to enjoy.

⚐ Assessment: Students should be able to correctly complete a food chain in their group and illustrate it in the correct sequence.
Use the "A Food Chain Comic Rubric" on page 123, "Worksheet Comics Rubric" on page 117, or the "Group Comic Activity Rubric" on page 115.

Examples of Food Chain labels for the name tags:

1. Mako Shark---Mackerel---Herring---Plankton
2. Lion---Antelope---Grass
3. Mountain Lion---Wolf---Rabbit---Vegetables
4. Mongoose---Cobra---Rat---Fruits & Vegetables
5. Polar Bear---Seal---Penguin---Shrimp
6. Grizzly Bear---Salmon---Insects

Historical Happenings
A Social Studies Activity

⚑ <u>Grade levels</u>: 3-6

⚑ <u>Time</u>: 1 to 2 class periods

⚑ <u>Lesson Plan Focus</u>: History

⚑ <u>Correlation to National Education Standards</u>

Social Sciences: Civics
NSS-C.K-4.2   Values and Principles of Democracy
NSS-C.K-4.5 and NSS -C.K 5-8.8   Roles of Citizens
World History Standards
Any of the National Standards for World History may apply depending upon the time period studied.
Language Arts Standards
NL-Eng.K-12.5   Communication Strategies

⚑ <u>Objectives</u>: After researching a historic event, students will accurately illustrate it in comic form.

⚑ <u>Preparing for the Activity</u>: Make a list of historical happenings for students to choose from to turn into a comic.

⚑ <u>Introducing the Activity</u>: Hand out copies of the comics from the daily newspaper. Allow time for students to read them. Then ask if any of these are set in another time period. Ask what type of clues the artist used to show this. Explain today's assignment will be for them to choose and do research about an event in history and then complete a comic that tells about what they have learned.

⚑ <u>Materials</u>
   Comics pages from the newspapers
   A copy of A Historical Happening template page for each student
   Pencils
   black "rollerball' ink pens
   erasers

⚑ Procedure

1. Hand out the copies of the Historical Happenings template page and go over it aloud.

2. Allow research time for each student. It will be important for them to decide which characters were most important in the event they have chosen, which might be left out, and the changes which occurred as a result of the event.

3. After completing their research, students should fill in the narration for their comic panels and draw their characters. Remind them they may add dialogue by writing the words and then drawing a caption bubble around them.

4. Finished comics could be displayed in chronological order on a bulletin board or wall.

⚑ Assessment
Use the "Worksheet Comics Rubric" on page 117.

_____
(Title)

A Historical Happening   by:_____

In the year_____,_____
_____

Some of the people
involved were :_____
_____

Before this event,_____
_____
_____

After this event,_____
_____
_____

Clip Art Comics
A Technology Activity

▶ <u>Grade levels</u>: 3-6

▶ <u>Time</u>: 1-2 class periods

▶ <u>Lesson Plan Focus</u>: Technology and Communication

▶ <u>Correlation to National Education Standards:</u>
Technology Standards
NT.K-12.1   Basic Operations and Concepts
NT.K-12.3   Technology Productivity Tools
Language Arts Standards
NL-ENG.K-12.4   Communication Skills
NL-ENG.K-12.6   Applying Knowledge
NL-ENG.K-12.8   Developing Research Skills
NL-ENG.K-12.12   Applying Language Skills

▶ <u>Objectives</u>: Students will find and use clipart from the internet or a clip art CD to create an instructional comic about computer usage.

▶ <u>Preparing for the Activity</u>: The teacher will need to find appropriate web sites for the students to look for clip art. Or, they will need CDs containing clip art images. Useful web sites are listed at the end of this lesson. You may want to add these to the "Favorites" list on the computers your students will be using.

▶ <u>Introducing the Activity</u>: Ask the class to help list some of the most important rules or guidelines to remember when they are using a computer. Write the list on the board. Guide the class to list the things you want them to practice when they are in computer lab, researching on the internet, working with a partner on the computer, etc. Then tell the class they are going to be creating a comic "Guide to Using a Computer." These can be funny as well as informative. Their comics may have one or two characters in them. Show an example if you have made one.

⚑ <u>Materials</u>
   Computers with printers
   Comic Panel Template page
   Scissors
   Glue
   Pencils, Ink pens
   Notebook paper
   Example of clip art comic made by the teacher

⚑ <u>Procedure</u>
1. Assign or have the students suggest a rule or guideline for using a computer that they would like to illustrate in a comic using clip art. Have them write the rule on a sheet of notebook paper.

2. Review, if necessary, how to access the internet or start a chosen program to find the clip art. If students work in pairs on this activity, you may want to have a timer so they both get to control the computer for equal amounts of time.

3. Finding the character(s) that will be in their comics will take students awhile. Because the focus of this lesson is on technology usage, allow plenty of time for this step.

4. When the characters have been found, the students should print several copies of the picture they have chosen. If the same character is shown in different poses, print those. These images may be saved and then taken into another artwork program so more than one image may be put onto one sheet of paper, thus conserving resources.

5. After the characters are printed, they should be cut out and glued onto the comic panel template page.

6. Students may use the sheet of notebook paper they used earlier to write out a script of what their characters will say. They should explain the rule or guideline for computer usage they chose earlier.

7. When the script is finished, it should be written on the comic, with the words being placed first, then the speech bubble being drawn around it.

8. This should be stressed so words are not squeezed in and unreadable.

9. The comics may be colored with colored pencils or left black and white.

10. Bind all of the comics together into a book, and have the class help name it as a book of guidelines for other students to read.

~Use this method of making a comic when you want to shorten the drawing process. It eliminates the student having to draw and redraw the same character several times for one comic. This might be very useful when working with handicapped students.

⚐ Assessment

The students' comics should make sense and illustrate the computer use guideline they chose. It should be legible and complete.
Use the "Clip Art Rubric" on page 119.

Check out these web sites for clip art:

http://free-clipart.net/mainhtml

http://www.free-graphics.com/main.html

CLIP-ART.COM@http://clipart.sitemynet.com/indexo.html

Fraction Comics
A Fraction Practice Activity

⚑ <u>Grade level</u>: 4-6

⚑ <u>Time</u>: One or two 45 minute classes

⚑ <u>Lesson Plan Focus</u>: To reinforce and apply the use of fractions.

⚑ <u>Correlation to National Education Standards</u>
Math Standards:
NM-MUM.3-5.1 & NM-NUM.6-8.1   Understanding Numbers, Ways of Representing Numbers, Relationships Among Numbers & Number Systems

⚑ <u>Objectives</u>: Students will correctly apply what they have learned about fractions by drawing comics illustrating fractions as they are directed. 80% accuracy will be expected.

⚑ <u>Preparing for the Activity</u>: Review the steps for creating a comic. Go over the comic vocabulary as needed.

⚑ <u>Introducing the Activity</u>: Cut comic strips from the Sunday newspaper to use as examples. Remind the students all of the panels together make one complete comic. Therefore, each panel in the comic represents a fraction of the whole. Show a comic strip, and ask questions such as, "What fraction of the comic panels contain a human? What fraction of the panels contains sound words? What fraction of the total panels contains an animal? " etc. Write these fraction answers on the board or the overhead and discuss as needed.

⚑ <u>Materials</u>
Blank panels page to draw the comics on, pencils and erasers, and the Fraction Comics Directions page.

⚑ Procedure

Explain that students will be following the directions given on the Fraction Comics Directions page to create their own comic strip. They will draw their comics on the blank panels page in pencil, paying close attention to the fractions given in the directions. Caution them that if the directions say that 2/3 of the panels should have speaking captions in them, they will have to be sure they don't have more or less. They may check each other's work as they go along.

⚑ Assessment

The teacher should review the students' work as they draw their comics. When the comics are finished, they should be checked to see if they have understood and correctly translated the fractions given and that these are represented in the drawings in their comics.
Use the "Worksheet Comics Rubric" on page 117.

⚑ Closure

Fractions are all around us. We use them every day, and they can be applied to many things, even the comics. Challenge students to come up with other applications for finding fractions in every day items.

⚑ Extensions

1. Make an assignment for students to cut a comic strip from the newspaper, and write ten fraction facts about the panels.
2. Send the student-drawn fraction comics to another class and have them write ten fraction facts about the panels. Those facts can be checked by the students who originally created the comics and the papers returned graded to the other class.
4. Have students create a large "Super Comic" collage by gluing panels from several different strips onto poster board. These can be arranged in any way the students like. (In this activity, the individual comic strips can be the fractional parts of the whole.) Then, have students complete a "survey" of the fractions in the comic, such as "1/4 of this super comic is composed of *Garfield,* 1/4 is made up of *Peanuts*, etc.
3. Teachers can make up their own fraction directions to go along with and review any subject area they may be teaching. For instance, the fraction practice could be combined with any curriculum by having the students draw panels including whatever is in the current chapter of study.
4. These comics may be finished by inking and coloring them and publishing them in a book that could be sent to lower grade levels.

Name_____

Fraction Comics Directions Page

Follow the directions given to create your own "fraction" comic.
Be sure to read carefully. And have fun!
In this comic, a sunny day will be turning into a rainy day. The characters in the comic will react to this change. Think about some simple things they could say, and keep this in mind while you are drawing.

1. Count the squares on your blank panel page. Write the total number of panels here: _____

2. You will be putting the title of your comic in the first panel. So, your title panel will be what fractional part of the entire comic? _____

3. Draw the sun in the background of 3 of the panels of your comic. The sun will be in 3/6, or 1/2 of your comic panels.

4. Draw clouds in the next to last panel. Clouds will be in what fraction of your total comic? _____

5. Show it raining in your last panel. What fraction of the total panels will it be raining in? _____

6. Choose an animal that will be your main character. Draw this animal in 5 of your panels. It can have different expressions and actions in the different panels. This character will be in 5/6 of your comic.

7. Now, add a new character to 4 of your panels. This character will talk to the other one you have already drawn. The new character will be in what fraction of your total comic? _____

8. Put a loud sound word in 1/6 of your comic. It should go along with the picture in the panel that you choose.

9. Have your characters speak to each other, and write what they are saying in caption bubbles.

10. Put the finishing touches on your comic and enjoy sharing it!

FRACTION COMICS

Invention Comics
A Research Activity

▶ <u>Grade level</u>: 3-6

▶ <u>Time</u>: 3-4 class periods

▶ <u>Lesson Plan Focus</u>:
Research, Writing, and Art

▶ <u>Correlation to National
Education Standards</u>
**All National Standards listed for
the "From Script to Comics"
lessons and:**
Language Arts Standards
NL-ENG.k-12.7   Evaluating Data
NL-ENG.k-12.8   Developing Research Skills
NL-ENG.k-12.12   Applying Language Skills
Science Standards
NS-k-4.5 & NS.5-8.5   Science and Technology
NS.5-8.6   Personal and Social Perspectives
NS.k-4.7 & NS.5-8.7   History and Nature of Science
Social Studies Standards
Individual to the invention studied and the time period in which it was created
Technology Standards
NT.k-12.5   Technology Research Tools

▶ <u>Objectives</u>: Students will do research about a certain invention, use this information to write their comic text, and produce a finished comic strip including the factual text and original drawings to illustrate it.

▶ <u>Preparing for the Activity</u>: Gather examples of everyday items with which students are familiar. The ball-point pen, paper clips, staples, and a zipper are easily found items. You may want to research and find the inventors of these items yourself to tell the class, or you may want students to help you look up that information as a warm-up activity.

▶ <u>Introducing the Activity</u>: Begin by having students name things they use every day and feel they could not do without. Then, ask them if they know who came up with the idea for these things. Explain these things are inventions, items thought up and then made because they filled a need in a useful way.

If possible, bring to class several out-dated inventions (or pictures of them), and ask the students if they know what those things were used for.

Materials

Resources for research	Drawing paper
Comic panel template page	Pencils
Black 'rollerball' ink pens	Colored pencils

Tell the class they will be researching an invention of their choice and doing a report about it. Then, add the report will be in the form of an informational comic strip. They will follow the steps they have already learned in the "From Script to Comic" lesson in this book.

Procedure

1. Have students write the name of their inventions at the top of a piece of paper. Once they have chosen, they should try to stay with subject unless they can't find any facts about it. Explain to students the facts should be written in paragraph form, and include when the item was invented, who invented it, and how it is used. This can be done in a 4-6 panel comic.

2. The paragraphs should be proofread and revised and rewritten. Then, the students must decide which parts of the story can be told in pictures, which parts of the story can be told in words.

3. A rough sketch of the comic is made, then proofread by the teacher and corrected again if necessary.

4. The final comic is drawn, outlined with black pen, and colored with colored pencils.

Assessment
The comic produced by the student should be factual and finished in a readable way that others can understand. You may want the students to share their comics aloud, in place of an oral report.
Use the "Student-Made Comics Rubric" on page 116.

Alien Election Comics
A Social Studies Activity

⚑ Grade level: 3-6

⚑ Time: 3-4 45-minute classes

⚑ Lesson Plan Focus: Social Studies/
              Electoral Process

⚑ Correlation to National
Education Standards
Social Studies Standards:
Civics NSS-C.5-8.2   Foundations of the Political System
NSS-C.K-4.3 & NSS-C.5-8.3   Principles of Democracy

⚑ Objectives: Students will create a comic showing their knowledge of the
Electoral Process.

⚑ Preparing for the Activity: Give each student a copy of the "Alien
Election" panel template and the "Create your own Alien" worksheet.

⚑ Introducing the Activity: Review the Electoral Process with your
students. Discuss the two-party system, the nomination process,
campaigning and "stump" speeches, and the election process. Discuss
vocabulary words such as; ballot, polls, campaign, nomination, candidates, etc.

⚑ Materials
    Copies of the "Alien Election" template
    Copies of Create Your Own Alien tutorial p. 108-109
    Blank sketching paper
    Pencils
    Erasers
    Ink pens (optional) Color pencils

⚑ Procedure
1. Tell students they will be creating their own comics depicting elections on
   an alien planet.

2. Distribute the "Create Your Own Alien" worksheet. Using pencils and
   sketch paper, instruct students to design their own alien characters and
   environments. They should create an Alien Reporter, an Alien Voter, and

two Alien Candidates. Also they need to create a name for their Alien Planet and two Alien Political Parties.

3. Pass out the "Alien Election" panel templates. Tell the students to fill in the blank spaces in the narration captions using their pencils.

4. In Panel 1, have the students draw their Alien Reporter and Alien Voter.

5. Solicit examples of the type of questions a reporter might ask and the response a voter might have. Tell them to add these words or those similar, into dialogue in speech balloons, above their characters in the first panel.

6. Then tell the students to add their background in Panel 1, where they have room. Do not let them start coloring yet.

7. Moving along to Panel 2, have the students draw their Alien Candidates. Next, discuss what these candidates might say when they are nominated. Then, have the students draw their characters, and add appropriate dialogue in speech captions. Finally, students can add background into their pictures. Encourage them to show different locations throughout their comics.

8. Discuss what candidates say in speeches and campaigns. Talk about "mudslinging," debates, and promises. Next, in Panel 3, have the students draw their two candidates debating or campaigning. Tell them to add appropriate dialogue inside speech captions. And then they can add their backgrounds.

9. In Panel 4, the students can show the winner or loser, celebrating voters, or a picture of the Alien City. They can add any appropriate dialogue inside speech captions.

10. After they have finished writing and drawing their comics, students can ink and then color their work. To save time, skip the inking process and simply make photocopies of the students' original comics. This will darken their lines and letters and keep their art work from smudging while they color.

⚐ Assessment

The teacher should visually check the students' work as they are doing the activity. The students' comics should show an understanding of the electoral process and vocabulary. Also, they should do their drawings and penmanship carefully to ensure clarity.

Use the "Worksheet Comics Rubric" on page 117.

⚐ Extension

Have the class create and hold their own "Monster Election." They can create monster masks, political parties, voters, and reporters. They can hold nomination parties, then hold debates, and do a mock election in which all of the Monsters vote for their favorite candidate.

ALIEN ELECTION

By: _____

On a distant planet named _____ an important election was in progress.

First the two political parties the _____ and the _____ chose their candidates.

Then the candidates began their speeches and debates.

Finally, the citizens of _____ chose their new leader.

Comic Graphs
A Graph Making Activity

🏴 <u>Grade level</u> – 3rd and up

🏴 <u>Time</u>: 1-2 Class Periods

🏴 <u>Lesson Plan Focus</u>
   Math, Creating a Graph

🏴 <u>Correlation to National</u>
   <u>Education Standards</u>
   Math Standards
   NM.NUM.6-8.1   Understand Numbers, Ways of Representing Numbers, Relationships Among Numbers and Number Systems
   Language Arts Standards
   NL-ENG.k-12.8   Developing Research Skills

🏴 <u>Objectives</u>: Students will decide upon a topic for their graphs, research to collect data, and present the data in graphs visually representing their findings.

🏴 <u>Preparing for the Activity</u>: Gather many different comic books. It could be helpful to send a note home to parents requesting help with this. The students will probably have comics they can bring from home, also.

🏴 <u>Introducing the Activity</u>: Show students an example of a graph, and have them explain what it is telling them. Ask the class, "Why would we want to use a graph to tell information instead of just writing it?" (A graph makes the information easier to see all at once.) Include other discussion that is grade appropriate.

🏴 <u>Materials</u>
   Large resource of age-appropriate comic books
   Typing or construction paper
   Pencils
   Crayons, markers or colored pencils
   Notebook paper

⚐ Procedure

1. Explain the information students will be using to create graphs will be found in comic books. They are to read several comics with a friend and then brainstorm ideas for collecting information from the books to create a graph.

2. Ideas for students to consider might be:
- Out of a total number of superheroes, how many have capes and how many don't?
- What are the most popular colors for superheroes' costumes to be?
- Compare the number of male superheroes to the number of female superheroes.
- How many comic characters wear glasses; how many don't?
- How many comic characters have a certain eye or hair color?
- Compare the number of funny comics with those that are serious.
- How many comic characters are animals instead of people?

3. When students have selected their graph topics, they will write their rough information on their notebook paper. They will need to decide which type of graph will best display their findings.

4. Using their research, students will create graphs. They should be correctly labeled and easy to understand. For younger students, you might want to assign a pictograph. For older students, a bar or pie graph might be good. Also, there are some good software programs, such as "Cruncher" for Mac computers allowing students to plug their information in, and create a graph they can print.

5. Display the graphs and show off the hard work.

⚐ Assessment
Use the "Comic Graphs Rubric" on page 121.

Acting Out
A Dramatic Activity

► Grade levels: 3-6

► Time: 1 class period

► Lesson Plan Focus: Communication and Creativity

► Correlation to National Education Standards
Language Arts Standards
NL-ENG.K-12.4   Communication Skills
NL-ENG.K-12.12   Applying Language Skills

► Objectives: Students will work in pairs or small groups to dramatize a comic.

► Preparing for the Activity: A large supply of comics will be needed for the students to choose from. Students may bring their own comics from home, if desired. The teacher should choose a comic they can act out for the class, and if needed, prepare a student to play a part also.

► Introducing the Activity: After finding a comic you can dramatize for the students, write it in script form. You may have to recruit a helper to play a part if there are two characters in your comic. Tell students you are going to put on a very short play for them. Act out the comic, and then show a copy of the original on the overhead for all to read. Could the students have guessed you were acting out a comic? Did they know which one it was? Show them the script you wrote from the comic on the overhead. Explain they will be turning a comic into words that they can act out, too. Tell them as an exercise in communicating with others they will be working with a partner to read, rehearse, and then act out a comic that they choose. This will give them an opportunity to be "in" their favorite comic and make it come to life.

⚑ <u>Materials</u>
Comics
Overhead transparencies of a comic and your script adaptation of that
    comic
Notebook paper and pencils
Construction paper, markers, and scissors for making props, if desired

⚑ <u>Procedure</u>
1. Each pair of students will need to carefully choose a comic to dramatize. Have them read it aloud to one another several times. They should try to imagine and portray how the characters would say the words. Remind them to practice expressions on their faces that go along with the words and what is happening in the comic.

2. Next, the students will each write their dialogue from the comic. If they have done the Scrambled Comics lesson, this will be easy for them. If not, it is good practice and something to recall later when writing comic scripts for another lesson. (If a chosen comic has 3 or more characters, other students may join the pair.)

3. It should be stressed when writing the dialogue (or script) for the comic, the words should be labeled with the name of the character who is speaking them.

4. Allow the pairs to practice, and if the students want to make props, this will take extra time but can be done very quickly. They should only try to make small things that are especially appropriate for the character and an important part of the comic.

5. Have the groups take turns presenting their plays. The students may take their scripts with them to read. This will make the nervous students more at ease. Have other students guess which comic strip the play is dramatizing.

⚑ <u>Assessment</u>
The students should be able to take the dialogues from their comics and turn them into scripts they can use to perform their plays. The dramatizations should be performed in a way the rest of the class can understand them. The importance of this lesson lies in getting those

students who are afraid to get in front of the class involved in a non-threatening way.

Use the "Group Comic Activity Rubric" on page 115 or the "Acting Out Rubric" on page 118.

⚑ Extension
~If students have created their own original comics, they could dramatize those instead of published comics.
~Have your class perform their plays for another class.

FYI
~There is a musical play called "You're a Good Man, Charlie Brown" dramatizing the comic strip by Charles Schultz.

Comics without Captions
An English Activity

▶ <u>Grade levels</u>: 3-6

▶ <u>Time</u>: 1 class period

▶ <u>Lesson Plan Focus</u>: Creative Writing
                              and Sentence Construction

▶ <u>Correlation to National Education Standards</u>
Language Arts Standards
NL-Eng.K-12.4   Communications Skills
NL-Eng.K-12.5   Communication Strategies
NL-Eng.K-12.6   Applying Knowledge

▶ <u>Objective</u>: Each student completes a comic by creating original captions correct in grammar, capitalization, and punctuation.

▶ <u>Preparing for the Activity</u>: Choose several comics from the Sunday newspaper. Choose one of these comics to make an overhead transparency. Then use correction fluid to cover the captions on all of the comics. Make another transparency of your chosen comic that has all of the words removed. Make copies of the comics without captions for your students to write on.

▶ <u>Introducing the Activity</u>: Show the transparency of your chosen comic <u>without</u> the words. Have students suggest words that could be put in the caption bubbles to complete the comic. Stress the words should match the expressions conveyed by the characters. Remind students they will be practicing good writing skills, and they will need to use complete sentences, check their spelling, and use correct punctuation. You may model this by filling in the captions with a marker with the students' suggestions. Next, show the transparency of the chosen comic as it originally appeared in the newspaper with the words intact. Compare this with what the class created.

⚐ <u>Materials</u>

    Transparencies - One of a chosen comic that has the original captions and
        another of the same comic with the words removed with correction
        fluid
    Copies of the comics you have removed the captions from
    Pencils and erasers
    Dictionaries

⚐ <u>Procedure</u>

1. Show the comics without captions pages to the students, and allow them
   to choose the one they want to work with. Tell them they may ADD
   caption bubbles as well as fill in the ones that are already shown on the
   comic.

2. Remind the students they are to complete the comics by filling in the
   captions with complete sentences that have correct spelling and
   punctuation. Also, the words must make sense with the pictures in the
   comic.

3. When finished, students should reread their own work to check for
   mistakes. Then they should ask a classmate to trade papers with them
   so they can check each other's accuracy.

4. For younger students, the teacher may want to proofread the captions
   for them and have students rewrite their sentences correctly.

Tip - This would be a great anchor activity for students who always get
finished early with their assignments. It is creative as well as good writing
practice.

Comic Collage
An Art Activity

⚐ <u>Grade levels</u>: 1st and up

⚐ <u>Time</u>: 3-5 class periods (Depending on the size of the project).

⚐ <u>Lesson Plan Focus</u>: Art - Collage and Sculpture

⚐ <u>Correlation to National Education Standards</u>
Visual Arts Standards

NA-VA.K-4.1 and NA-VA.5-8.1	Understanding and Applying Media, Techniques, and Processes
NA-VA.K-4.2 & NA-VA.5-8.2	Using Knowledge of Structures and Functions
NA-VA.K-12.3 & NA-VA.5-8.3	Subject Matter, Symbols, and Ideas

⚐ <u>Objectives</u>: Students will work cooperatively to create a large shape that is covered with comics that are specific to the project. The shape will be made to either hang on the wall, hang from the ceiling, or to be free-standing. The teacher will decide upon the size of the finished project.

⚐ <u>Preparing for the Activity</u>: Accumulate comic books and comics from the newspaper to cut up to use in the collage. Find photos showing sculpture work done by Alexander Calder.

⚐ <u>Introducing the Activity</u>: Show the students examples of artwork by the artist Alexander Calder, who used bold shape and color to create beautiful and well-balanced mobiles and stabiles. Discuss the shapes he chose and why he chose them.

⌘ <u>Materials</u>

Books with examples of work by Alexander Calder

Comic books and newspaper comics

Large pieces of cardboard or foam core board

A large sheet of butcher paper for each group

Box or Exacto® knife for the teacher to use

Scissors

Glue

Paint (for the back of the shape if it isn't hung on the wall)

Mod Podge® or other water-based varnish and sealant

Cardboard box (to attach the collage to for a free-standing sculpture)

String to hang the finished piece, or hot glue and glue gun, or a box if the piece is to be free-standing

⌘ <u>Procedure</u>

1. Divide the class into small groups of five or six. Allow them to look through the comics and choose their favorite.

2. Have the groups decide upon a shape representing their comic in some way. For example, a large bat could be the background for a Batman comics collage, a large spider for Spiderman comics, a large Snoopy shape for Charlie Brown comics, etc.

3. Give the students the butcher paper, and tell them they will be making the pattern for their large shape on it that will be the background for their comic collage. For younger students, you may want to have the shapes already cut out and guide them to the comics that would be used to cover it in collage. Older students will be able to create a pattern for their background shape for you to apply to the cardboard and cut out with a box or Exacto® knife. (This could be the end of the first class period for the activity, and the teacher could cut out the shapes out of class.)

4. If the teacher chooses to cut out the background shape in class, the students can use this time to find and cut out comics to cover the shape.

5. Demonstrate how to use the Mod Podge® or other collage glue/sealer to affix the comics onto the background to create the collage. The placement and direction of the comics may be important, and the neater the work, the better the overall appearance of the piece will be.

6. Allow students to work on the collage. Stress the importance of gluing all edges down well and of completely covering the entire background with pictures. The teacher will need to monitor this.

7. When the collages are dry, the backs will need to be painted if they are to hang from the ceiling. To hang heavy pieces, first punch holes in the top of the collage, and then use a large paper clip tied onto kite string to attach it to the ceiling. The string may be tied to the metal divisions used to support ceiling tiles. If you have a different type of ceiling, you may need to place screws into the ceiling, and tie the kite string to those. If the collages are to hang on a wall, the use of hot glue may be helpful, because masking or grey tape will not hold them up for long.

If the collage is to be free-standing, a cardboard box could be attached to the back with hot glue to keep it upright. (Put a brick or other weight in the box if needed for balance.)

⚑ Assessment
The student groups should plan and complete a comic collage to put up for display. It should be neatly done, and the background should be completely covered.
Use the "Comic Collage Rubric" on page 120.

The "Save the World" Game
A Creative Review Activity

⚑ <u>Grade level</u> - 3rd and up

⚑ <u>Time</u>: 3-4 class periods

⚑ <u>Lesson Plan Focus</u>: Comics Review & Assessment and Cooperative Problem Solving

⚑ <u>Correlation to National Education Standards</u>

Language Arts Standards
NL-ENG.k-12.8   Developing Research Skills
Visual Arts Standards
NA-VA.k-4.1 & NA-VA.5-8.1   Understanding & Applying Media, Techniques, and Processes

⚑ <u>Objectives</u>: The students will create their own games using comic trivia. The games must be playable by others in the class and provide a review or evaluation of information that has been previously taught.

⚑ <u>Preparing for the Activity</u>: Have some samples of board games for the students to look at and get ideas from.

⚑ <u>Introducing the Activity</u>: Ask the class how many of them have ever played a trivia game. Many will say they have. Ask them if the questions are easy or hard. Ask if they can see how playing a trivia game would be like taking a test at school. Have them compare the two.

⚑ <u>Materials</u>
    11" x 17" sheets of white paper (or two 9"x 12" pieces, taped together)
    150 - 3" x 5" file cards (or, six for each student)
    Crayons and markers
    Notebook paper
    1 sheet of white construction paper for each child
    Dice- enough for each group to have one

⚐ <u>Procedure</u>

1. Hand out one sheet of notebook paper to each student. Explain you will be reviewing the information they have learned, and the quiz will be in the form of a game. Not only that, but the students will actually be making up the questions for the quiz.

   Tell the class to think hard and to formulate six good questions each about the comics' unit you have studied. Specify they may only write questions they know the answers to.

2. Divide the class into groups of four. Since these students will be working together to make a game from their questions, they may not have any duplicate questions on their list.

3. Collect these papers, check for accuracy of questions and answers, and hand back. Then have the students copy their questions onto file cards. These will be the cards for their games.

4. Next, have students make their playing pieces. Hand out pieces of white construction paper 1" x 4" in size that have been folded in half to make them 1" x 2". (This fold-over is so the playing piece can stand up.) The students are to create their own superhero comic characters and color them on one side of the folded paper.

5. Hand out 2 sheets of white construction paper to each group of four. They should tape it in the middle so it will fold. A winding path should be drawn to create a game board, with squares large enough to accommodate the playing pieces. A "start" space should be labeled, and the ending space should be a picture of the world with "Save the World" written on it.

6. Duplicate and give each group a copy of the "Directions for Play" page. This will make finishing the construction of the game much easier.

7. The group must label some of the squares on the board with instructions such as "You can fly. Go ahead 2 spaces" or "Your superhuman strength takes you ahead 3 spaces" or "An evil villain ties you up. Lose 1 turn."

8. Then they will color and decorate the board.

© Pieces of Learning

9. Some of the squares will have to be labeled "Super Trivia" or something similar, so the students' trivia questions will be used.

When the game boards are finished, students can play their games and have fun while they are reviewing information.

⚐ Assessment
The teacher should circulate among the groups as they are playing their games, and observe how they are answering the trivia "review" questions. Use the "Save the World Game Rubric" on page 125 or the "Group Comic Activity Rubric" on page 115.

⚐ Extensions
~ Use this game for an assessment at the end of any subject unit.

Save the World Game - Directions for Play

Pieces of the Game: One die, a playing piece for each player, the game board and the Super Trivia question cards.

Purpose of the Game: To move your Superhero playing piece through the hazards of the game board and to reach the "Save the World" space first.

Movement: All players will roll the die and the one with the highest number will move first. After that, play moves around the group to the right of the first player.
On a turn, each player will roll the die and move the number of spaces shown. They will follow the directions written on the squares they land on.

"Super Trivia" Squares: If a player lands on a Super Trivia square, he or she should draw a card, and hand it to another player to read aloud. If the question is answered correctly, the player does nothing but will move on his next turn. If he answers incorrectly, then he will lose his next turn.

Winning: The player who reaches the "Save the World" square at the end of the board wins. You do NOT have to roll the exact number to land on this square. The winner gets to stand up and say, "I saved the world!" if she wants to and takes the bows she deserves as a true superhero.

Explain any other special instructions here:_____
_____
_____
_____

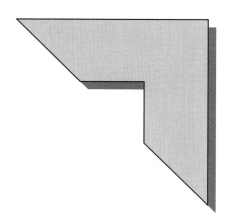

Worksheets
&
Assessment Tools

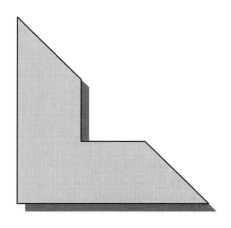

Comic Story Templates

The next few pages are templates students can complete to create their comics. Each could be used in several curriculum areas. Below are explanations that go with each page taking the teacher step-by-step through helping students complete the comics.

Use of appropriate dialogue should be stressed, and sound words should be encouraged.

For each comic the title will need to be designed and added by the student.

The Hungry Child Comic Template

In this comic, the student will create a character, fill in narration and dialogue, and solve a problem.

First panel:
A child should be shown walking and talking about how they feel about being hungry.

Second panel:
The child discovers a fruit tree, but it is taller than they are, and they cannot reach the fruit.

Third panel:
The child finds something native to the forest he or she can use to solve the problem of reaching the fruit.

Forth panel:
The child is shown enjoying the fruit he or she has gotten.

The Horrible Noise Mystery Comic

The student will create at least one character, show a confrontation with something scary, and develop a good conclusion.

First panel:
The picture is complete except for the writing.

Second panel:
Here the student has to picture his or her own character reaching over to turn on the light and looking around. A scared expression is important to show.

Third panel:
This panel shows the confrontation of the character and the source of the mysterious noise.

Forth panel:
The conclusion is shown.

The Day at the Dump Comic

The student will create two characters and a strange object, provide completed narration, write dialogue, and show the characters' reactions.

First panel:
The two characters should be shown playing a game or exploring at the city dump.

Second panel:
The characters find an object.

Third panel:
The characters react to what the object is doing.

Forth panel:
The results of the object's activity are shown.

(Title)

by: _____

Just as _____ was beginning to
            NAME
drift off to sleep, _____ heard
                    he/she
a horrible noise ...

screeeK

"

SCRATCH SCRATCH

_____ quickly reached over
    NAME
and turned on the lamp.

click

thump
thump

In the bright light _____ saw
                     he/she
_____
_____

With the mystery solved,
_____ decided to _____
    NAME
_____.

(Title)

By:_____

One day _____ and _____
were playing at the dump.

They discovered a _____
and _____ object.

Suddenly the object began
to _____
_____
_____

Then, they realized what
the object was...

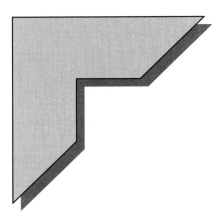

Blank Panel
Templates

Included in this section are many blank panel templates for use in your classroom. There is one Comic Strip template and several Comic Page templates. Choose the appropriate templates for the lessons. Or you can create your own blank panel templates.

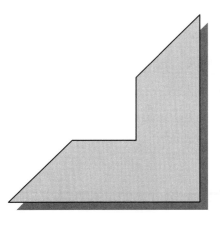

Drawing Handouts for Students

In this section you will find resources for your students. There are handouts showing the creative process of comics. And there are handouts with many drawing lessons. Share these fun and informative pages with your students.

Many of these lessons are easy to do. Try some yourself!

-Comics Vocabulary

-Creating Comics

-From Script to Comics

-Heads

-Detains

-Emotions

-Hair

-Bodies

-Aliens

-Bubble Letters

-Panel Layouts

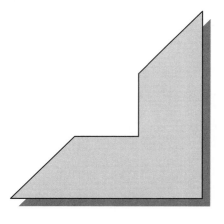

COMICS VOCABULARY

COMICS – PICTURES AND WORDS USED TOGETHER TO **SHOW & TELL** A STORY, IDEA, POEM, OR JOKE

PICTURES – DRAWINGS OR OTHER IMAGES USED TO SHOW A STORY, IDEA, POEM, OR JOKE

WORDS – LETTERS GROUPED TOGETHER IN ORDER TO TELL A STORY, IDEA, POEM, OR JOKE

PANELS – THE VARIOUS SHAPES THAT CONTAIN THE PICTURES IN A COMIC

PANEL LAYOUT – THE GROUPING OF PANELS ON A COMIC PAGE OR STRIP

GUTTERS – THE EMPTY SPACES THAT SEPARATE THE PANELS OF A COMIC

CAPTIONS – THE VARIOUS SHAPES THAT CONTAIN AND DISTINGUISH THE WORDS IN A COMIC

TAILS – THE POINTERS THAT ISSUE FROM CAPTIONS IDENTIFYING THE SPEAKER, THINKER OR SUBJECT OF A COMIC

PANEL

PICTURE

CAPTION

TAIL

GUTTER

WORDS

COMIC PAGE

COMIC STRIP

OPEN PANEL

HOW TO DRAW THE CAPTIONS

1. I'M HUNG

2. I'M HUNGRY.

3. I'M HUNGRY.

TIP: KEEP THE LETTERS FROM TOUCHING THE BALLOONS.

SPEECH CAPTIONS

HI!
I'M HUNGRY!
LOOK! UP IN THE SKY.
OUCH!
HMM... I WONDER.

THOUGHT CAPTIONS

WHO CARES?
SHOULD I GO LEFT OR RIGHT?
I HATE THE RAIN.

NARRATION CAPTIONS

LATER THAT NIGHT...
SUDDENLY...
ALL DAY, CLARA WAITED FOR HER DOG TO RETURN. WHILE SHE WAS WAITING....

SOUNDS – "ONOMATOPOEIA"

TAP TAP TAP
BAM
SQUISH
CRRREEEAK~
DING DONG
POP

CREATING COMICS

FIRST, WRITE YOUR NARRATION WORDS AT THE TOP OF THE PANEL.	NEXT, DRAW YOUR CHARACTERS INSIDE OF THE PANEL....	THEN, WRITE YOUR SPEECH WORDS ABOVE THE CHARACTERS....
On a distant world named Sniknej...	On a distant world named Sniknej... 	On a distant world named Sniknej... What is your opinion, sir? It stinks! 

TIP: WHEN YOU DO YOUR SPEECH WORDS, REMEMBER TO FIRST WRITE THE WORDS, AND THEN DRAW THE BALLOONS AROUND YOUR WORDS.

NEXT, DRAW YOUR BACKGROUND. START WITH A HORIZON LINE.	THEN ADD THE BASIC SHAPES. TRY NOT TO DRAW INTO YOUR WORDS.	FINALLY, ADD ALL OF THE DETAILS INTO YOUR BACKGROUND.
On a distant world named Sniknej... What is your opinion, sir? It stinks!	On a distant world named Sniknej... What is your opinion, sir? It stinks! 	On a distant world named Sniknej... What is your opinion, sir? It stinks! 

NOW YOU ARE READY TO BEGIN WORK ON THE NEXT PANEL OF YOUR COMIC!!

FROM SCRIPT TO COMICS

FOLLOW THESE STEPS WHEN YOU ARE READY TO TURN YOUR STORY INTO A COMIC.

❶ THE WRITTEN STORY

- STARTING WITH A BLANK PIECE OF PAPER, WRITE YOUR OWN STORY.
- TRY TO MAKE IT 4-8 SENTENCES LONG
- MAKE SURE THAT YOUR STORY HAS A BEGINNING, MIDDLE, AND END.
- GIVE YOUR CHARACTERS SOME UNIQUE AND INTERESTING DETAILS.
- CREATE A TITLE FOR YOUR STORY
- DO NOT DRAW ANY PICTURES YET, THAT IS FOR THE NEXT STEP.

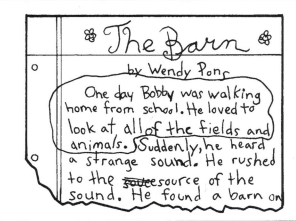

❷ THE ROUGH DRAFT COMIC

- STARTING WITH A BLANK PANEL TEMPLATE, COPY THE FIRST 1 TO 2 SENTENCES FROM YOUR WRITTEN STORY TO THE INSIDE OF THE FIRST STORY PANEL.
- KEEP THESE WORDS AT THE TOP OF THE PANEL.

  DRAW A LINE TO SEPARATE THESE WORDS FROM YOUR PICTURES.
- KEEP YOUR PICTURES ROUGH. NO DETAILS YET. TRY USING STICK PEOPLE, OR ONLY OUTLINES.
- ADD SOME DIALOGUE FOR THE CHARACTERS TO SAY.
- FINISH THE NEXT 3 PANELS OF THE ROUGH DRAFT.

❸ THE FINAL DRAFT COMIC

- WHEN YOU FINISH YOUR ROUGH DRAFT COMIC, GET A NEW BLANK PANEL TEMPLATE.
- COPY ALL OF YOUR WORDS & PICTURES FROM THE ROUGH DRAFT TO THE FINAL DRAFT.
- WHEN YOU COPY THE WORDS, DO YOUR BEST PENMANSHIP. ALSO, WATCH YOUR SPELLING AND GRAMMAR.
- WHEN YOU COPY THE PICTURES ADD LOTS OF DETAILS. DRAW CAREFULLY & CLEARLY.
- MAKE SURE THAT NONE OF YOUR DRAWINGS INTERFERE WITH YOUR WORDS.

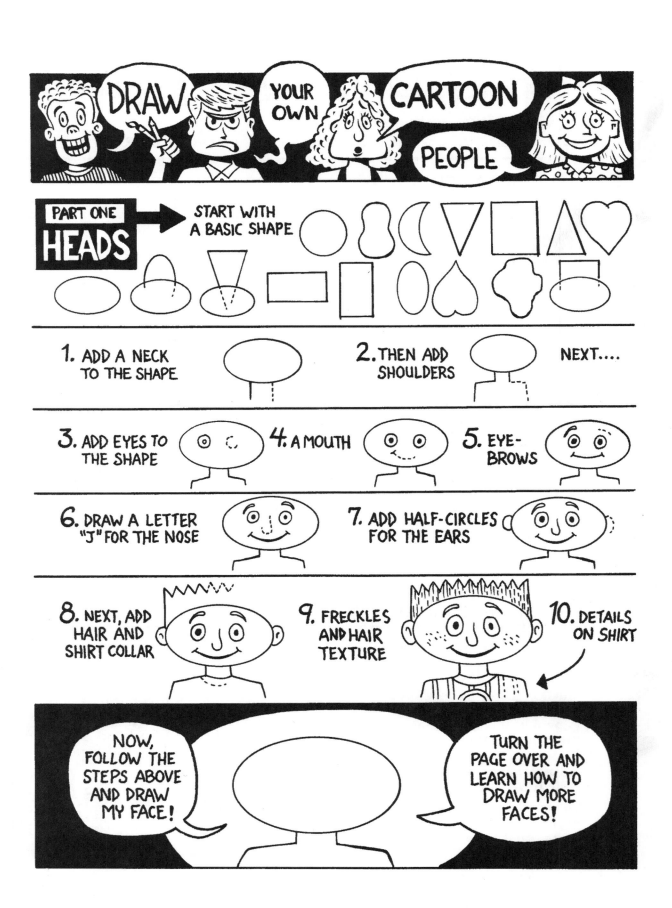

PART TWO DETAILS!

EACH ONE OF YOUR CHARACTERS SHOULD LOOK DIFFERENT. AS THE ARTIST, IT IS YOUR JOB TO GIVE EACH CHARACTER INTERESTING AND UNIQUE DETAILS. TRY SOME OF THESE IDEAS.

SOME DIFFERENT KINDS OF NOSES.

LETTER "J" NOSE	LETTER "L" NOSE	"ANIME" NOSE

SOME DIFFERENT KINDS OF EARS.

CIRCLE EARS	PEANUT EARS	SQUARE EARS

DETAILS INSIDE OF THE EARS

1. 2.

WHEN YOU DRAW GIRLS, ADD SOME EYELASHES. BE CAREFUL! TRY NOT TO LET THEM TOUCH THE EYEBROWS.

TRY SOME GLAMOROUS LIPS, TOO!!

1. 2. 3. 4.

HERE ARE MORE DETAILS THAT YOU CAN ADD TO YOUR OWN CHARACTERS.

FACIAL HAIR

SCAR

BAND AID

FRECKLES

JEWELRY

PART THREE
EMOTIONS

MOST OF OUR FEELINGS ARE CONVEYED WITH OUR EYES, MOUTH, AND EYEBROWS. AS YOU DRAW YOUR COMIC, TRY TO SHOW LOTS OF DIFFERENT EMOTIONS.

HAPPY	AMUSED	MAD	ENRAGED	SCARED	TERRIFIED	EMBARASSED
GLAD	CONTENT	ANGRY	FRUSTRATED	NERVOUS	SHOCKED	GUILTY
LAUGHING	LOVESTRUCK	ANNOYED	IRKED	HEARTBROKEN	INFURIATED	SAD
EXCITED	SURPRISED	WRATHFUL	UPSET	SNEAKY	MANIACAL	BORED

ADD ANY OF THESE EXPRESSIONS TO A BASIC SHAPE. THEN YOU CAN ADD EARS, NOSE, AND OTHER UNIQUE DETAILS TO YOUR CHARACTER'S FACE.

CREATE FUN WAYS TO **EXAGGERATE** YOUR CHARACTER'S EMOTIONS.

PART FOUR
HAIR!

 FOLLOW THESE STEPS TO CREATE DIFFERENT KINDS OF HAIRSTYLES FOR YOUR CHARACTERS. REMEMBER TO MAKE EACH OF YOUR PEOPLE LOOK DISTINCTIVE.

1. FIRST, DRAW THE HEAD & FACE....

2. THEN DRAW THE OUTLINE OF THE HAIR

3. NEXT.... ERASE

4. ERASE THE EXTRA LINES & ADD TEXTURE

TRY THESE **DIFFERENT** HAIRSTYLES. LOOK FOR THE DOTTED LINES. THESE LINES ARE PART OF THE ORIGINAL HEAD SHAPE. ERASE THEM AS YOU FINISH DRAWING THE HAIR.

PART FIVE
BODIES!

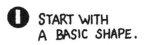

F OLLOW THESE STEPS TO CREATE THE BODIES FOR YOUR CHARACTERS. REMEMBER TO ALWAYS START WITH BASIC SHAPES & THE ADD THE DETAILS.

1 START WITH A BASIC SHAPE.

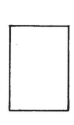

LEAVE ROOM FOR THE HEAD & LEGS.

2 ADD THE LIMBS. MAKE THE ARMS AND LEGS AS LONG AS THE BODY.

3 ADD FEET, HAND, AND HEAD SHAPES.

ERASE

4 THEN ADD THE FACE HAIR AND CLOTHING.

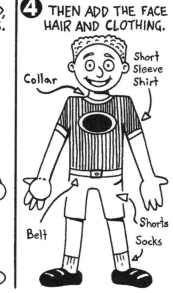

Collar

Short Sleeve Shirt

Belt

Shorts

Socks

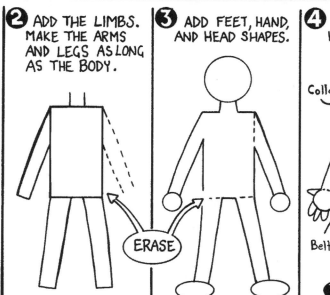

DRESS

1.　2.　3.　ERASE　4.　DECORATE

COAT

1.　2.　3.　4.

COLLARS

1.　2.　3.

1.　2.　3.

F OLLOW THE STEPS ABOVE AND DRAW YOUR OWN CHARACTER.

N OW TURN THE PAGE OVER TO LEARN HOW TO DRAW MORE BODIES!

106

© Pieces of Learning

BODIES CONTINUED

Ⓣ HE BODY MOVES IN MANY WAYS. SHOW WHAT YOUR CHARACTERS ARE DOING & HOW THEY FEEL.

ELBOWS   KNEES   NECK   SHOULDER

Ⓤ SE DIFFERENT SHAPES AND SIZES TO ADD VARIETY TO YOUR CHARACTERS. ALSO, MAKE THEIR DETAILS & CLOTHING DISTINCTIVE. **BE CREATIVE!!**

WALKING
1. 2. 3. 4.

CLIMBING STAIRS
1. DRAW STAIRS FIRST
2.
3.
4.

SITTING
CHAIR FIRST
1. 2. 3. 4.

CREATE YOUR OWN ALIEN

1 START WITH A BASIC SHAPE FOR THE BODY AND THE HEAD.

2 NEXT, DECIDE WHAT KINDS OF LIMBS YOUR ALIEN WILL HAVE.

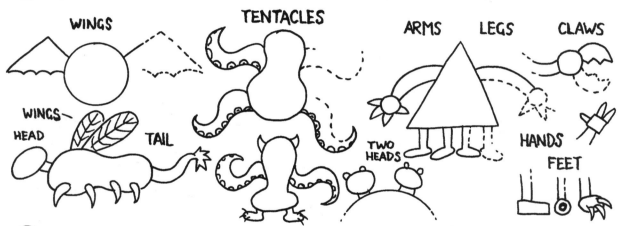

WINGS
TENTACLES
ARMS   LEGS   CLAWS
WINGS
HEAD   TAIL
TWO HEADS
HANDS
FEET

3 THEN, DESIGN YOUR ALIEN'S FACE AND ADD COOL DETAILS!!

HORNS   ONE EYE   ANTENNAE

108

4 HERE ARE SOME EXAMPLES OF ALIEN BACKGROUNDS. USE THESE FOR INSPIRATION WHILE YOU ARE CREATING YOUR ALIEN COMICS!

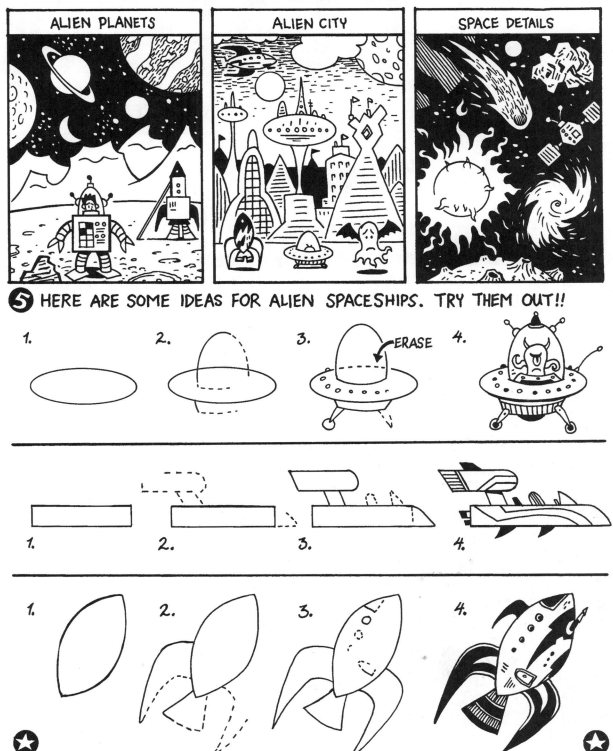

| ALIEN PLANETS | ALIEN CITY | SPACE DETAILS |

5 HERE ARE SOME IDEAS FOR ALIEN SPACESHIPS. TRY THEM OUT!!

1.   2.   3. ERASE   4.

1.   2.   3.   4.

1.   2.   3.   4.

ADD BUBBLE LETTERS INTO YOUR COMICS TO MAKE SOUND EFFECTS AND TITLE DESIGNS. FOLLOW THESE STEPS TO CREATE THEM.

① LIGHTLY DRAW YOUR WORD. MAKE YOUR LETTERS TALL AND LEAVE SOME SPACE IN BETWEEN.

B L A M !

② BEGIN TO DRAW AROUND EACH LETTER......

BLAM!

③ ERASE THE LINES INSIDE OF THE BUBBLE LETTERS....

BLAM!

④ ADD THE "HOLES" INSIDE OF THE LETTERS... "△"

"D" → BLAM!

SOME LETTERS THAT WILL NEED "HOLES" (△ D O Q Q)

A→A B→B D→D O→O P→P Q→Q R→R

TRY SOME DIFFERENT STYLES OF LETTERING. REMEMBER TO START WITH STEP #1 ABOVE. HAVE FUN!!

BLOCK LETTERS

BUBBLE LETTERS

SHOCK LETTERS

SCARY LETTERS

DRIPPING LETTERS

PUFFY LETTERS

BUBBLE LETTERS CONTINUED·

SOUND EFFECTS & TITLE DESIGNS

ADD SOUND WORDS TO ENHANCE THE STORYTELLING IN YOUR COMICS. TRY TO MAKE YOUR LETTERS **LOOK** LIKE THEY SOUND AND FEEL.

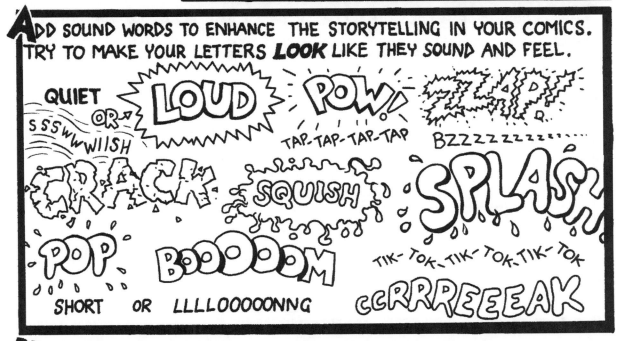

QUIET OR — SSSWWWIISH — LOUD — POW! — ZZZAP!
TAP-TAP-TAP-TAP — BZZZZZZZZZZ...
CRACK — SQUISH — SPLASH
POP — BOOOOOM — TIK-TOK-TIK-TOK-TIK-TOK
SHORT OR LLLLOOOOONNG — CCRRREEEAK

USE BUBBLE LETTERS WHEN YOU CREATE YOUR TITLE DESIGNS. ALSO, ADD PICTURES AND DECORATIONS TO JAZZ THEM UP!

CAT'S PAW
BY: Wendy Pons
THESE LETTERS ARE FUZZY, LIKE THE HAIR OF A CAT.

CAT'S PAW
By- Wendy Pons
THIS DESIGN INCLUDES A PICTURE OF THE MAIN CHARACTER.

CAT'S PAW
By: W. Pons
A PATTERN OF PAW PRINTS IS INCLUDED IN THIS TITLE.

CAT'S PAW
By- W. Pons
TRY DECORATING YOUR TITLES WITH STRIPES OR POLKA DOTS!

PANEL LAYOUT

THE GROUPING OF PANELS ON THE PAGE OF A COMIC IS CALLED THE PANEL LAYOUT. BELOW ARE SOME DIFFERENT LAYOUTS THAT YOU CAN TRY ON YOUR OWN COMIC. THE GRID LAYOUT IS THE EASIEST LAYOUT TO USE. ALSO, THE GRID LAYOUT IS THE ONE WITH THE MOST ROOM FOR THE WORDS AND PICTURES OF YOUR COMIC.

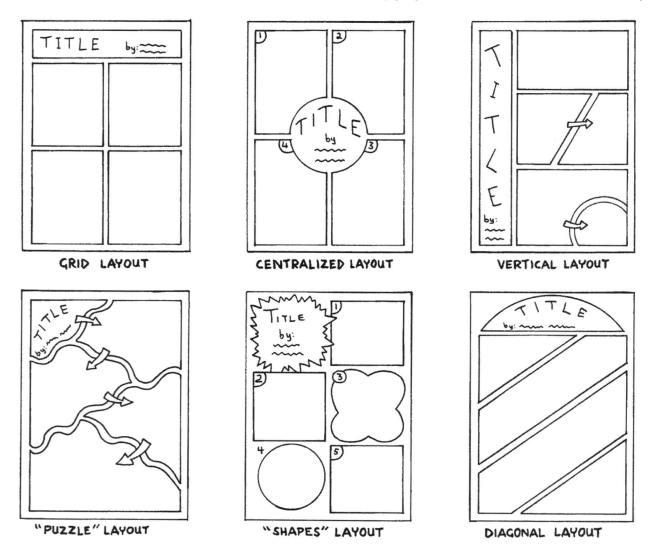

GRID LAYOUT

CENTRALIZED LAYOUT

VERTICAL LAYOUT

"PUZZLE" LAYOUT

"SHAPES" LAYOUT

DIAGONAL LAYOUT

REMEMBER THAT OTHER PEOPLE WILL BE READING YOUR COMIC. SO, IF YOU CREATE AN UNUSUAL LAYOUT, HELP THEM BY USING ARROWS OR NUMBERS ON YOUR PANELS.

THE GRID LAYOUT IS THE EASIEST PANEL LAYOUT FOR MOST PEOPLE TO READ.

THE JOB OF THE CARTOONIST IS TO BE BOTH **CREATIVE** AND **CLEAR**. HAVE FUN!

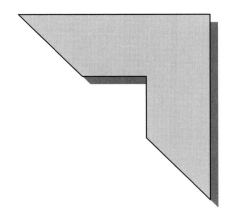

Rubrics

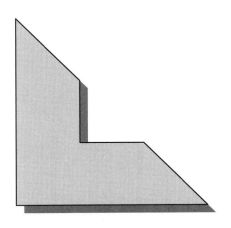

Rubrics for
"Comics in Your Curriculum"

In this section you will find rubrics for assessing your students work. You can match each rubric with their corresponding lesson plan by noting the titles. We have also included two *generic* rubrics for assessment of multiple lessons found in this book.

The "Worksheet Comics Rubric" could be used to evaluate any of the following activities:

Historical Happenings
Fraction Comics
Alien Election Comics
And any of the Comic Story Templates at the back of the book.

The "Student-Made Comics Rubric" could be used with any of these activities:

From Script to Comics
Explain That Operation
Invention Comics

The "Group Comic Activity Rubric" might be used with any activity where the teacher has students work in cooperative groups to create a comic instead of assigning individual projects.

This rubric would work well with the following lessons:

Superphonics
A Food Chain Comic
Acting Out
Comic Collage
The "Save The World" Game

Remaining lessons have their own rubrics on the following pages.

Group Comic Activity Rubric

Skills	1	2	3	4	Points
Helping The teacher observed the students offering assistance to each other.	*None* of the time	*Some* of the time	*Most* of the time	*All* of the time	
Listening The teacher observed the students listening to and working from each other's ideas.	*None* of the time	*Some* of the time	*Most* of the time	*All* of the time	
Participating The teacher observed each student contributing to the project.	*None* of the time	*Some* of the time	*Most* of the time	*All* of the time	
Persuading The teacher observed the students exchanging, defending, and rethinking ideas.	*None* of the time	*Some* of the time	*Most* of the time	*All* of the time	
Questioning The teacher observed the students interacting, discussing, and posing questions to all members of the team.	*None* of the time	*Some* of the time	*Most* of the time	*All* of the time	
Respecting The teacher observed the students encouraging and supporting the ideas and efforts of others.	*None* of the time	*Some* of the time	*Most* of the time	*All* of the time	
Sharing The teacher observed the students offering ideas and reporting their findings to each other.	*None* of the time	*Some* of the time	*Most* of the time	*All* of the time	
				Total Points	

Names of group members

_____
_____
_____
_____
_____

Grading Scale

A = _____ points
B = _____ points
C = _____ points
D = _____ points

Student-Made Comics Rubric

Name _____

Objectives	1	2	3	4	Points Earned
The student will complete a story to put in comic form.	The story is incomplete.	The story is complete and contains a beginning, middle and end.	The story is complete, has a beginning, middle, and end, and has been proofread and corrected with the help of the teacher.	The story is complete and has a beginning, middle, and end, has been proofread and corrected by the student.	
The student will Make a multi-panel comic from their story.	The comic contains some elements of the written story.	The comic displays some student knowledge of substituting pictures and captions for words in the story.	The comic displays student knowledge of substituting pictures and captions for words and using dialogue correctly in the panels.	The comic displays student knowledge of substituting pictures and captions for words and using dialogue in the panels. All errors have been corrected.	
The student will ink the penciled comic and finish it.	The comic has not been entirely traced over with ink.	The comic has been traced over with ink, but is messy.	The comic has been traced over with ink and pencil lines have been erased. The page is neat and clean	The comic has been traced over with ink and pencil lines have been erased. The page is neat and clean, and the comic has been finished in color.	
			.	**Total**	

116

© Pieces of Learning

Worksheet Comics Rubric

Name _____

Objectives	1	2	3	4	Points Earned
The student will complete the narration on the worksheet to show knowledge of the subject, and make up captions with dialogue that includes specified content.	The captions do not include content that was assigned. The dialogue does not add to the understanding of the subject.	The captions and/or the dialogue do not completely show understanding of the subject and the content that was assigned.	The captions and the dialogue show understanding of the subject and the content that was assigned. The work was not proofread well.	The captions and the dialogue show an excellent understanding of the subject and content required. The work has been proofread and corrected.	
The student will make appropriate drawings to complete the comic.	The pictures in the comic do not go along with the text in the narration and the dialogue.	The pictures in the comic sometimes go along with the text in the narration and the dialogue.	The pictures in the comic go along with the text in the narration and the dialogue and help to clarify the text.	The pictures in the comic are neatly drawn, they go along with the text and clarify it. The pictures add to the content of the information given.	
The student will ink the penciled comic and finish it.	The comic has not been entirely traced over with ink.	The comic has been traced over with ink, but is messy.	The comic has been traced over with ink and pencil lines have been erased. The page is neat and clean.	The comic has been traced over with ink and pencil lines have been erased. The page is neat and clean, and the comic has been finished in color.	
			.	**Total**	

Acting Out Activity Rubric

Name _____

Criteria	1	2	3	4	Points
Collaboration With Peers	Rarely listens to, shares with and supports the efforts of others in the group. Does not seem to value teamwork.	Often listens to and supports others in the group, but is not a good team member.	Usually listens to, shares with, and supports the efforts of others in the group. Does not cause problems in the group.	Almost always listens to, shares with, and supports the efforts of others in the group. Works to make things go smoothly.	
Preparedness	Student does not seem prepared and has to be helped through the presentation.	The student is somewhat prepared, but needed some help.	Student seems fairly well prepared.	Student is completely prepared.	
Enthusiasm	Very little use of expression or body language. Did not generate much interest in the presentation.	Facial expressions and body language are used somewhat.	Facial expressions and body language generate some interest in the presentation.	Expressions and body language generate strong interest in the presentation, and the student acts with enthusiasm.	
Presentation of Material	The presentation was not relative to the comic material used.	The presentation was somewhat relative to the comic material being used.	The presentation was relative to the comic material being used.	The presentation was extremely relative to the comic material being used.	
				Total Points	

Names of group members:	Grading Scale
_____ _____ _____ _____ _____ _____	A = _____ points B = _____ points C = _____ points D = _____ points

Clip Art Comics Rubric

Name _____

Criteria	1	2	3	4	Points
Graphics Choice	Graphics were not appropriate to the comic and/ or they were of poor quality.	Graphics were somewhat appropriate to the comic and/ or they were of fair quality.	Graphics were appropriate to the comic and/or they were of good quality.	Graphics were very appropriate to the comic and/or they were of high quality.	
Completion of Computer Rule or Guideline	The assignment was less than 69% completed, or it was done very poorly.	The assignment was 70-79% completed.	The assignment was 80-89% completed.	The assignment was 90-100% completed.	
Comic Script	The comic script was not understandable and/or it contained many errors..	The comic script was only somewhat understandable and/or it contained some errors.	The comic script was understandable but it contained some errors.	The comic script was understandable and it contained no errors.	
Neatness and Organization	The work is sloppy and disorganized. It is hard to read.	The work is organized, but is hard to read.	The work is organized and usually easy to read.	The work is well organized and always easy to read and understand.	
Documentation of Illustration Sources	Documentation was not given for the illustrations used.	Documentation was given for some of the illustrations used.	Documentation was given for almost all of the illustrations used.	Documentation was given for all of the illustrations used.	
				Total Points	

Names of group members:

_____
_____
_____
_____
_____
_____

Grading Scale

A = _____ points
B = _____ points
C = _____ points
D = _____ points

Comic Collage Rubric

Name _____

Criteria	1	2	3	4	Points
Attention to Theme	The student cannot explain how the items in the collage relate to the theme. (Or there is no theme.)	The student has difficulty explaining how the items in the collage relate to the theme.	The student gives a reasonable explanation of how the items in the collage relate to the theme.	The relationship of the items to the theme of the collage is for the most part clear and needs little explanation.	
Creativity	The student did not creatively alter any of the items used in the collage.	The student creatively altered one or more items in the collage.	The student creatively altered more than 3 of the items in the collage.	The student used an exceptional degree of creativity in their collage by altering and customizing several items on the collage.	
Design	Graphics or items are untrimmed or are of inappropriate size or shape. Little planning was put into the design of the work.	Graphics have been trimmed to an appropriate size, but there was little planning in the design of the work. Added items do not work well in the design.	Graphics have been trimmed to an appropriate size and shape and have been arranged with planning. Items have been placed with a plan in mind. However, the work does not appear balanced.	Graphics have been trimmed, are appropriate in shape and size, and have been arranged into a balanced and meaningful design. Added items work well in the design.	
Time and Effort	Class time was not used wisely. Little effort was put forth, and the work is unfinished.	Class time was not always used wisely, but the work was finished.	Class time was used well; the student took some time to plan and complete the work.	Class time was used well; the student took extra time and effort to complete the work in an excellent way.	
Quality of Construction	The collage was not put together well; some pieces or items are loose. Glue use was messy and shows on the work in several places.	The collage was put together fairly well, with only a few pieces or items having loose edges. There are a few smudges of glue showing.	The collage was put together well, with 1 or 2 pieces or items having loose edges. Only a few smudges of glue are showing.	The collage was put together and it shows that extra attention was given to the construction. No pieces or items are loose, there are no glue smudges showing.	
				Total Points	

Grading Scale

A = _____ points
B = _____ points
C = _____ points
D = _____ points

Comic Graph Rubric

Name _____

Criteria	1	2	3	4	Points
Graph Topic	Graph topic was not appropriate to expression in graph form	Graph topic was difficult to express in graph form	Graph topic was appropriate, and lent itself to expression in graph form.	Graph topic was an excellent choice for expression in graph form.	
Gathering of Data	Necessary research was not done.	Some research was done, but not nearly enough.	Data needs to be backed up with more research.	Research was well done and is well represented in the graph.	
Type of Graph Chosen	Graph does not represent the data well and is confusing or difficult to understand.	Graph does not represent the data well and is somewhat difficult to understand.	Graph is adequate to represent the data, but is a little difficult to understand.	Graph fits the data well and makes it easy to understand.	
Neatness and Attractiveness	Graph is messy and "thrown together" in a hurry.	Graph is complete but is quite plain looking.	Graph is neat and relatively attractive. It is very readable.	Exceptionally well designed, neat and attractive. Colors go well together and make the graph more readable.	
Title and Labeling	A title is not present and/or labeling is not complete.	The title is present, but is not capital-ized or does not state the topic of the graph. Labeling is not complete.	The title clearly states the topic being graphed and is at the top of the graph. Labeling is complete.	Title is creative, states the topic being graphed, is at the top and is neatly done. Labeling is excellent.	
				Total Points	

Grading Scale

A = _____ points
B = _____ points
C = _____ points
D = _____ points

Explain That Operation Rubric

Name _____

Criteria	1	2	3	4	Points
Representation of Mathematical Concepts	Explanation shows limited understanding of the math concept chosen for representation in the comic.	Explanation show some understanding of the math concept chosen for representation in the comic.	Explanation shows substantial understanding of the math concept chosen for representation in the comic.	Explanation shows complete under-standing of the math concept chosen for representation in the comic.	
Use of Mathematical Terms	There is little use of math terms, or they are used incorrectly.	Correct math terms are sometimes used, but their meanings are not always clear.	Correct math terms are usually used, making it fairly easy to understand what was meant.	Correct math terms are always Used, making it easy to understand what was meant.	
Mathematical Errors	There were more than 3 errors in the explanation of the math problem.	There were 3 errors in the explanation of the math problem.	There were 2 errors in the explanation of the math problem.	There was no more than 1 error in the explanation of the math problem.	
Neatness and Organization	The work is sloppy and disorganized. It is hard to read.	The work is organized, but is hard to read.	The work is organized and usually easy to read.	The work is well organized and always easy to read and understand.	
Comic Illustrations	The comic illustrations are difficult to understand and do not go well with the content of the comic.	The comic illustrations are somewhat difficult to understand and go with the content of the comic fairly well.	The comic illustrations are easy to understand and go well with the content of the comic.	The comic illustrations greatly add to the understanding of the content of the comic.	
				Total Points	

Names of group members:

_____
_____
_____
_____
_____

Grading Scale:

A = _____ points
B = _____ points
C = _____ points
D = _____ points

A Food Chain Comic Rubric

Name _____

Criteria	1	2	3	4	Points
Correct Sequence of Food Chain	The food chain was not correctly grouped by the students. The teacher had to correct it.	The food chain was not correctly grouped by the students, but they were able to fix their mistake.	The food chain parts were grouped correctly, but they were in the wrong sequence.	The food chain parts were grouped correctly and they were in the correct sequence.	
Illustration of the Food Chain	The illustration is incorrect or it is unrecognizable.	The illustration is done correctly but it is very messy..	The illustration is done correctly.	The illustration is done correctly, very carefully, and neatly.	
Comic Strip	The pictures are not in the correct order in the comic strip.	The comic strip is done correctly but is very messy.	The comic strip is done correctly.	The comic strip is in the correct order and shows creativity in the way the food chain is represented.	
Narration and Dialogue	Narration and dialogue are hard to read and show many spelling and/or grammatical mistakes.	Narration and dialogue show some spelling and/or grammatical mistakes.	Narration and dialogue are fairly easy to read and have very few spelling or grammatical mistakes.	Narration and dialogue are very easy to read and have no spelling or grammatical mistakes.	
				Total Points	

Grading Scale

A = _____ points
B = _____ points
C = _____ points
D = _____ points

History of Comics
Internet Scavenger Hunt Rubric

Name _____

Criteria	1	2	3	4	Points
Student's Internet Usage	Was unable to log on or navigate on the internet without constant help.	Was unable to log on or navigate on the internet without some help.	Was able to log on and navigate on the internet with only a little help.	Was able to log on and navigate on the internet with no help.	
Correct Completion of the Assignment	Student completed the assignment with 69% or less of the answers correct.	Student completed the assignment with 70-79% of the answers correct.	Student completed the assignment with 80-89% of the answers correct.	Student completed the assignment with 90-100% of the answers correct.	
Staying on Task	Student did not stay on task and went to websites other than those they were instructed to. use.	Student stayed on task some of the time, but went to websites other than those they were instructed to use.	Student stayed on task most of the time, but went to websites other than those they were instructed to use.	Student stayed on task all of the time and did not go to websites other than those as they were instructed to use.	
Time Management	The student did not finish the assignment in the allotted time.	The student finished 80% of the assignment in the allotted time.	The student finished 90% of the assignment in the allotted time.	The student finished 100% of the assignment in the allotted time.	
				Total Points	

Grading Scale

A = _____ points
B = _____ points
C = _____ points
D = _____ points

Save the World Game Rubric

Name

Criteria	1	2	3	4	Points
Accuracy of Content	Several of the information cards made for the game have in-correct information.	Two or three of the information cards made for the game are not correct.	Only one of the information cards made for the game is not correct.	All of the information cards made for the game are accurate.	
Attractiveness	Two contrasting colors were not used, and there are fewer than 3 graphics.	Two contrasting colors were used and printed graphics were added to the game board and cards.	At least two contrasting colors were used and 1 or more original graphics were created for use on the game board and the cards.	At least two contrasting colors were used and 3 or more original graphics were created to add to the appeal of the game board and cards.	
Cooperative Work	The group often disagreed and did not work together well. The game appears to be the work of one or two in the group.	The group worked fairly well together. All members seem to have contributed to the game.	The group worked generally well together. And was well organized .All members contributed quality work.	The group worked extremely well together, was organized and all members contributed equal amounts of quality work.	
Game Directions	The game directions were not written out. (Or were not completed.)	The directions were written, but others had difficulty understanding them.	The directions were written, but some needed to be slightly modified for better understanding.	The directions were clearly written, with no corrections necessary. They were easily understandable and complete.	
Creativity and Completion	The game was not finished.	The game was finished, but little thought was put into making it interesting or appealing.	The game was finished, some thought had been put into making it interesting, and attention was put into adding creative touches.	The game was finished, much thought had been put into making it interesting, and extra effort was put into adding creative touches such as special playing pieces and other decorations that added to the fun of game play.	
Grading Scale A = _____ points B = _____ points C = _____ points D = _____ points				**Total Points**	

Name _____

Criteria	1	2	3	4	Points
				Total Points	

Name _____

Criteria	1	2	3	4	Points
				Total Points	

About the Authors

Richard Jenkins is a professional comic book creator and illustrator. In 1994, Richard earned his BFA in Painting from the University of Oklahoma. Upon graduation he began pursuing the publication of his comic book projects and working as a freelance illustrator, creating magazine & CD covers, characters designs, and storyboards for television commercials. 1996 marked the beginning of his career as the illustrator and co-creator of the *Sky Ape* comic book series. Since then he has created many comic books and graphic novels.

Since 1997 Richard has also been working as an Artist-in-Residence with the Arkansas, Oklahoma, and Utah Arts Councils. He brings his knowledge and expertise into the classroom, teaching students of all ages how to create their own comics, drawings, and paintings. He has also led many professional development workshops for teachers across the country, training them how to teach their students the process of cartooning and drawing and how to integrate other curricula into the projects.

Samples of his work, and his students' artwork, can be seen at his web site: **www.studiohijinx.com**

Debra Detamore has been a classroom teacher in the Moore Public School District in the state of Oklahoma since 1987. She is currently working in the Gifted Education program in that district, and has served on the Gifted Education Advisory Committee. Debra holds a BA in Art Education K-12, and a teaching certificate in Elementary Education from the University of Central Oklahoma.

Ms. Detamore has presented workshops at several district and state level conferences including OAGC (Oklahoma Association of Gifted and Creative) and Encyclomedia. Her collaboration with Richard Jenkins began in 2002.

Debra has created and taught many professional development workshops for the Moore School District. She is especially interested in developing curriculum that makes it easy for teachers of all subjects to integrate art into their classrooms.

Both Teachers have tested lessons in this book at workshops and in the classroom.